The
JOY
of the
SECOND
COMING

The JOY of the SECOND COMING

by Hugh F. Pyle, D. D.

SWORD OF THE LORD PUBLISHERS
Murfreesboro, Tennessee 37133

Printed and bound in the U.S.A.

Dedication

This book is dedicated to Dr. Lee Roberson of Chattanooga, Tennessee. Years ago when I was directing a camp in west Florida, we invited Dr. Roberson to be our camp speaker for the week. He was impressed with a song, "Some Golden Daybreak," which we were using as one of the camp songs each evening. I believe it furnished the theme and title for his own excellent book on the second coming.

The joy of the second coming of Christ has permeated the powerful preaching of Dr. Roberson. I have heard some of the world's greatest preachers in the Bible Conferences at Highland Park Baptist Church and Tennesee Temple University, and I am so grateful to Dr. Roberson for allowing me to hear such men. These men of God confirmed what I had already learned from the Word about the glorious return of Christ.

I do not believe I have ever heard Dr. Lee Roberson speak without his mentioning and rejoicing in the thrilling theme of the second coming. He has been a great inspiration to me and to my ministry through the years, as he has been to thousands of preachers everywhere.

So with many thanks this book is affectionately dedicated to DR. LEE ROBERSON!

Table of Contents

Preface

The book of Revelation comes to life in the chapters of this book, *The Joy of the Second Coming.* Could His return be very near? What is the Great Tribulation? Will World War III destroy our civilizaton? What is Armageddon, and when will it take place? Will Christians be caught away from this earth in a secret rapture? Are the events described in Revelation to be taken literally? What about the Mark of the Beast? Are the H-Bomb and nuclear war predicted in the Bible? How can a knowledge of these truths transform the life? How do you reconcile seemingly contradictory verses about the return of the Lord? What is the secret of being joyful and optimistic in times like these?

The answers will be found in this book. Read it, then share its message with others.

As often is the case, there will be some quotes, poems, points and illustrations that I have picked up along the way without remembering where they came from. Or maybe I never did know. But I am grateful to preacher friends, authors and others who have contributed to what the Lord has given me for this book. Thanks to all faithful proclaimers of prophetic truth who have been my inspiration to love His appearing and to share the thrill and joy of the second coming with others.

My special thanks to Mrs. Beth Myers Hollis who has faithfully typed the manuscripts for this book (and others) graciously, and cheerfully, as unto the Lord! God bless you, Beth!

—The Author

CHAPTER 1

The Coming Great Event in History

It may happen very soon! The Lord Jesus Christ is coming to this earth again.

One verse in every twenty in the New Testament tells us that Jesus is coming again. And those who have counted the verses to prove it declare that there are more verses in the Old Testament relating to His second coming than there are concerning His first coming. If He came on time the first time, we have every reason to believe that He will keep His word and come on time the second time. A tiptoe expectancy is created throughout the entire Bible pointing to this great event of the second coming of Jesus Christ.

The first promise in the Bible is found in Genesis 3:15, often called the seed-plot of the Bible. Here God tells us that the seed of the woman, the virgin-born Messiah, the Son of God, will one day bruise the head of that old serpent, the Devil. And Romans 16:20 reminds us that that bruising of Satan will take place at the second coming of Jesus Christ.

The last promise in the Bible (Rev. 22:20) reads, "Surely, I come quickly."

The last prayer in the Bible is John's cry, "Even so, come, Lord Jesus."

Dr. I. M. Haldeman was, for many years, pastor of the First Baptist Church of New York City. He was a great prophetic preacher. Lines of people waited outside his church on Sunday evenings in Manhattan, hoping to get in, waiting for a seat to hear his sermons on the second coming of Christ. These messages, they say, lasted on an average of 1 hour and 45 minutes per sermon! Dr. Haldeman's book, *Ten Sermons on the Second Coming,* is a classic in prophetic literature, one of the greatest books on prophecy ever written. In this book, Dr. Haldeman stated (concerning the imminent, premillennial return of Christ), "You cannot read your Bible intelligently without an understanding of this glorious truth."

Yes, the whole Bible will make sense if you have an understanding of the truth of His sure return. And to understand the Bible correctly is the only answer to what is happening in the world today.

A missionary friend of mine in Mexico recently wrote lamenting the fact that we see each other so seldom, and he said, ". . .but we each have a job to do. And it may soon be all over. This old world is rapidly parading down Prophecy Boulevard in a death dance that amazes me." That's mighty well put. In this book you are going to see many of the things that are happening on Prophecy Boulevard. You will be able to read your Bible intelligently, and you will understand the book of Revelation far better.

Could we even now be entering the Great Tribulation? Will World War III destroy our civilization? Is the end of the world near? What is Armageddon, and when will that happen? Will this world be invaded from outer space? Is there a secret rapture when Christians will be caught away from coming judgment? What will happen to those who are left behind? All of these questions, and many more, will be answered before you finish reading this book.

As there is a scarlet thread running from Genesis to Revelation to tell us of Jesus' blood, so there is a golden thread running from Genesis to Revelation to tell us that Jesus is coming again. Perhaps we have gotten so busy wondering what the world is coming to that we have forgotten who is coming to the world! Yes, the Son of God is coming back to this earth, and it may be very soon!

Have you wondered why Egypt, Ethiopia, Libya, Syria, and

Lebanon are being mentioned with regularity on the evening news? These nations were almost forgotten for centuries; now suddenly they are in the news every day. It is no accident that Russia has invaded Afghanistan and that we have been embroiled in a confrontation with Iran. Truly, the armies of the world are being gathered around Palestine in the Middle East (see Luke 21:20).

The world cries for peace, but the Bible reveals there will be no peace until the Prince of Peace returns to this earth. After a year in office, President Jimmy Carter was being applauded by some world leaders as "a world superstar." One year later there was much pessimism and great gloom about the possibility of Mr. Carter's peace efforts. Shortly after that he went down to terrible defeat in the next presidential election, and another "superstar" of peace was gone!

The book of Revelation points to a one-world government and a world dictator. How significant then that today we have on every hand constant efforts toward super government, the United Nations, the common market, the ecumenical movement, the unisex movement, world education, and even a one-world church. All of this is significant! And it all coincides with the computerized society that is unfolding today.

In Matthew 24:3 the disciples came to Jesus saying, "Tell us, when shall these things be? and what shall be the sign of thy coming, and of the end of the world?" Then Jesus proceeded to answer them with words that sound almost as if they were written last week concerning events that are transpiring today.

The first thing He mentioned was false christs and false prophets in verses 5 and 11. Those who will come saying, "I am Christ" shall "deceive many" (Matt. 24:5). And verse 11 speaks of many false prophets that shall rise and deceive many. So, we have Mr. Moon of Korea with his moon madness, Hare Krishna, transcendental meditation, Armstrongism, Mormonism, Jehovah's (false) Witnesses, and many other "isms" and "wasms" and "spasms" that abound today.

A black charlatan stands on the platform in the largest auditorium in the city of Atlanta crying, "Money, honey! Just send me your tithes and offerings and you, too, can drive around in a gold-plated Cadillac." He chuckles sinfully as he speaks of his mistresses and his high living. He scoffs at the old-time religion and the salvation of the Bible, urging people to send him their tithes and offerings in order to prosper spiritually. Multitudes, of course, have done just this.

In an unprecedented ecumenical gesture some time ago, a recent pope invited forty U. S. Episcopal and Canadian Anglican clergymen to celebrate a Protestant mass in the Vatican. A Protestant *mass?* A thing like that would have been totally unheard of or unthought of just a few short years ago. Things are happening so quickly now as the one-world government is beginning to take shape and the integrated, ecumenical world church is shaping up.

Next, Jesus spoke of wars and rumors of wars (Matt. 24:6). You do not need me to tell you that we do not get out of one war before we get into another. Before his decease, Einstein cried, "The human race stands in imminent danger of perishing agonizingly. Those who know the most are the most gloomy about the possibility of the survival of the human race."

Recently I was in a meeting in Omaha, Nebraska, and a young Air Force officer took me out to Offut Air Force Base and down into SAC (Strategic Air Command) Headquarters. I sat in the balcony overlooking the control room where men are constantly watching the map of the world with the blinking lights in preparation for World War III. I heard their conversation with others over the hotline telephones as they engaged in conversation with Norad, with the Pentagon, and with various installations.

I sat where many of the generals will be sitting and perhaps where the President of the United States will be sitting, if they are still around after the first foreign missiles hit us. I went down under the three floors of concrete past several steel doors, signing in three times, and giving my Social Security number before armed guards in order to get into SAC Headquarters. Even there, of course, they know they are not completely safe from a direct hit by an atomic missile. I saw the red telephones to the White House and to the Kremlin.

It is an eerie thing to think about. There is a possibility that they can intercept Russian bombers, but the missiles they fear most and those atom-carrying submarines are out there in waters around the United States even today. It is not known how many of them may be poised and pointed towards America from Cuba, just 90 miles off the Florida coast. Once the missiles are launched, there is no stopping them. We are getting ready for World War III. And we are being told that Russia is far ahead of us in preparedness!

In verse 7 Jesus spoke of famines. It is hard for us to believe here in lush, fat, well-fed America that there are millions starving or suffering from malnutrition. A United Nations report on world hunger recently revealed that a half billion of the world's people go to bed hungry each night. How close could we be to famine even here in America?

In Detroit some time ago during the truckers' strike, after only a little over a week, we were being told in the Detroit newspapers that certain food items would not be on the shelves in the supermarkets after a few days of the truckers' strike continued, that certain other food items would soon become scarce.

I have flown over the Mississippi Delta when it was flooded and looked at thousands of acres of lush vegetable and fruit lands under water—ruined! I think of the corn blight in the midwest some time ago, of the chicken disease in Texas and Idaho, of a deep citrus freeze in Florida, of the peanut and other crops ruined in the summer of 1980 from that terrible drought.

Now just suppose that a merciful God allowed many of these events to take place at the same time! Can you imagine what it would be like? If events like the corn blight, the chicken disease, the flooded vegetable lands, the frozen citrus and the truckers' strike all coincided, we could be going up and down back alleys looking for a scrap of food in garbage cans in a matter of a few short weeks.

Jesus spoke also of pestilences. Do you know that there is a venereal disease epidemic among teenagers in America today?

And there is one strain of VD that is humanly incurable. Millions of people have this terrible social disease for which they can find no cure. We are told that the pain and sores will remain forever. God has fixed it so that people just do not live in sin and get away with it; and so we have this pestilence of disease. There are also many viruses and almost every year a new strain of flu. These are pestilences. And have you ever heard of so many people dying of cancer? It is epidemic in the world today, particularly in our well-fed, more civilized societies.

Earthquakes are happening, just as Jesus predicted in Matthew 24:7. When I was a boy, one hardly ever heard of an earthquake. Once or twice a year perhaps you read of one occurring. But eight years ago, when I left the pastorate, earthquakes were increasing in frequency and intensity. I look at some recent headlines: Pakistan—death toll from an earthquake—4,700. Massive "quake shakes Turkey"—1,300 die. In Guatemala—thousands died in an earthquake. Northern Italy—hundreds perished in an earthquake. And then China, Russia, Turkey, the Philippines, Rumania, Iran and Yugoslavia—thousands were killed in these earthquakes. Even as this book is being written, we are receiving the fearful news of the thousands who died in another earthquake in Italy in late 1980. They are still uncovering the bodies. God continues to let His alarm clock go off to remind us of His divine displeasure with the sins of this world.

California lives with "quake fear," we're told. Other parts of America are called "earthquake country." And scientists believe we will soon have some tremendous earthquakes in America. Verse 12 of Matthew 24 reveals that "because iniquity shall abound, the love of many shall wax cold." Iniquity (sin) is certainly abounding on every hand today. Barbarians are butchering one another not in the so-called heathen lands but in the night clubs and homes and streets of American cities. No man in his right mind would let his wife or daughter walk down the streets of a modern city after dark unescorted.

Some time ago, the television news in Washington revealed that 800 to 1,000 rape victims are counted every year in our nation's capital. That is probably only the tip of the iceberg as great numbers of rape victims never report the incident. A number of large American cities seem almost to be competing for the title of "murder capital" of the U. S. A. Elderly people are crying for more protection. One old gentleman in Cleveland states that he is afraid to go to the store for aspirin lest he be mugged or killed. A great number of children were recently murdered in Atlanta, Georgia. Six innocent people were shot to death in a bakery in Connecticut.

In Washington, D. C., some time ago, Human Kindness Day was celebrated. Jeffrey Hart reminds us that the name was ghoulishly inappropriate. On the day in question, some 125,000 people turned up at the Washington Monument for a concert by Stevie Wonder, a blind rock star. There then transpired an orgy of violence with strong racial overtones. Roaming bands of ghetto toughs were the aggressors. Hundreds of people went to the hospital. Rapes, robberies, and savage beatings took place in broad daylight. One participant in Human Kindness Day had his right eye put out by an ice pick. While all this was going on, the huge crowd remained largely passive, and the District of Columbia police did little to help the victims or restrain the toughs. One witness talked with a cab driver who saw a white girl slugged and kicked around while several policemen stood idly by. It was later reported that the District of Columbia police had specific orders not to act against blacks committing acts of violence. The official view was that the police were too few in number to handle a race riot if police action precipitated one, and this was probably true.

Certainly here we see the fulfillment of II Timothy 3:1, ". . .in the last days perilous times shall come."

And speaking of bloodshed and violence, it has been lately revealed that the legal killing of the unborn in the District of Columbia now outnumbers live births by roughly two to one. None of the other major cities could match this percentage of abortions to births. Surely we will one day give an account to a holy God for the deliberate killing of millions of unwanted and unborn children.

These are but a few of the many things pointing to the possible soon return of the Son of God to this earth scene. This is the coming great event in human history. Liberal theological unbelievers despise the truth of His coming, and ungodly worldlings would like to ignore and forget it. Sadly, even many Christians have neglected to learn the wonderful truths of the Bible concerning the second coming of the Saviour. Nothing has to take place before Christ could come in the air for His own. The Bible reveals that He will one day descend from Heaven with a shout (I Thess. 4:16) and that He will take away (rapture out) of this world those individuals who have personally received Christ as Saviour and thus have become the children of God.

Acts 1:11 in the Bible states that this same Jesus, who was taken up from the disciples from Galilee's shore forty days after His resurrection, will come in like manner as they saw Him go into Heaven. They stood there with their mouths open, gazing in wonder as the Son of God literally ascended in His physical but glorified body before their very eyes. He had just given them the Great Commission and final words of counsel before He took off for Heaven; and the Bible states that He is now seated at the right hand of the Father, making intercession for God's children and awaiting the day when He will return to take unto Himself His own.

In the Upper Room, in John 14, before Christ was taken in the Garden of Gethsemane by the Roman soldiers, He said to His chosen ones, the true believers, "Let not your heart be troubled: ye believe in God, believe also in me. In my Father's house are many mansions: if it were not so, I would have told you. I go to prepare a place for you. And if I go and prepare a place for you, I will come again, and receive you unto myself; that where I am, there ye may be also" (Vss. 1-3).

So He promises to come back for His bride, the true church, for a heavenly honeymoon yet future. The Bible teaches that He will come "as a thief in the night," and we know that a thief does not do the courtesy of telling us exactly when he will arrive so that we can leave the right rear bedroom window open and the silver out. In other words, the return of Christ for His own will be secret and unexpected as to the actual time.

No man can know the day nor hour when the Son of God returns, the Bible declares. Revelation 22:12 tells us that He will come quickly and His reward will be with Him to give to every man according as his work shall be. So the second coming of Christ relates to true believers, and those who are saved by trusting in Christ are encouraged to be ready and faithfully serving Him so we will not be ashamed before Him at His coming (see I John 2:28).

> Some golden daybreak, Jesus will come;
> Some golden daybreak, battles all won,
> He'll shout the vict'ry, break thru the blue,
> Some golden daybreak, for me, for you.
>
> —Carl A. Blackmore

"I *will* come again," the Saviour promised. The writer of Hebrews states, "For yet a little while, and he that shall come will come, and will not tarry" (Heb. 10:37).

The coming of Christ for His own and the events surrounding it are referred to as "the day of Christ," while the personal return of Christ in glory all the way back to the earth is referred to as "the day of the Lord." There will be a brief period of time between the rapture, or day of Christ, and the revelation of Christ at the day of the Lord. At the rapture, He will come in the clouds and cry, "Come up hither" (Rev. 4:1); "Rise up, my love, my fair one, and come away" (Song of Sol. 2:10). Saved people will then be caught up to meet the Lord in the air before the Great Tribulation begins upon this earth. The Great Tribulation is the time of unprecedented judgment when God's wrath is poured out upon a Christ-rejecting world and He deals in a particular way with the Jew. This time is referred to in Jeremiah 30, verse 7, as "the time of Jacob's trouble."

At the end of the tribulation, climaxed with the Battle of Armageddon, Christ will come back all the way to the earth, not just in the clouds above the earth. When He comes to the earth at the revelation, He will come with ten thousands of His saints (Jude 14), then will be fulfilled the prophecy of Isaiah, "For, behold, the Lord will come with fire, and with his chariots like a whirlwind, to render his anger with fury, and his rebuke with flames of fire. For by fire and by his sword will the Lord plead with all flesh: and the slain of the Lord shall be many" (Isa. 66:15, 16).

At the day of the Lord, Revelation 1:7 will be fulfilled, "Behold, he cometh with clouds; and every eye shall see him, and they also which pierced him: and all kindreds of the earth shall wail because of him. Even so, Amen."

It is plain to see that this second phase of the coming of Christ relates to the unsaved, for Paul writes to the Thessalonians, ". . . the Lord Jesus shall be revealed from heaven with his mighty angels, In flaming fire taking vengeance on them that know not God, and that obey not the gospel of our Lord Jesus Christ: Who shall be punished with everlasting destruction from the presence of the Lord, and from the glory of his power" (II Thess. 1:7-9).

The first thing for you to be sure of as we think about prophecy and the return of the Lord is our preparation for that great event. Are you prepared?

Many thrilling events will be studied and dealt with in this book as they relate to prophecy, the return of the Lord, and the book of Revelation. But the prophetic truths of the Bible are not for speculation and entertainment. The solemn promise of His sure return should be an urgent reminder to the unbeliever to make sure that he has found an evacuation route before the wrath of God falls upon a Christ-rejecting, God-hating, Bible-despising generation. On the outskirts of large cities as we travel around America in our motor home, we frequently see the sign, "Evacuation Route." This is the road so designated as an escape route from the cities in the event of some terrifying disaster or catastrophe. I found my evacuation route when I trusted Christ as my Saviour. It is straight *up*, and I am waiting with eagerness for the Lord's sure return!

CHAPTER 2

My Trip Into Outer Space

During the past sixteen years, history has recorded a number of trips into outer space. In rockets and space capsules men have gone to the moon and beyond.

A Long Island man sometime ago laid claim to a crater on the moon and was selling space at $1.00 an acre. He had accumulated $9,000 before the authorities stopped him! Many people seem to be itching to get into outer space. During the Cuban missile scare, it is said that people were contacting travel agencies inquiring about possible evacuation to the moon. Some wit has wondered if mail service from the moon would possibly be a little faster than from some parts of the good old U. S. A.!

One thing a Christian knows for sure—he is soon to take a trip into outer space.

My trip into outer space will be a *THRILLING* trip. It will be without rocket or plane or space capsule.

My trip into outer space will be a *TRANSFORMING* trip. The Bible declares in Philippians 3:21 that this vile body of our humiliation will be fashioned anew like unto His glorious body. We will experience a wonderful transformation on the way up into outer space.

My trip into outer space will be a *SPEEDY* trip. First Corinthians 15:51 tells us that it will take place in a moment, in the twinkling of an eye (vs. 52). Yes, faster than the speed of sound we will be whisked up for our heavenly honeymoon with the divine Bridegroom.

It will be a *SAFE* trip. Cape Canaveral has been called by some "Malfunction Junction," because of all the things that can go wrong in plans for a space voyage from this earth. However, when the Lord comes back, our trip into outer space will be a perfectly safe trip. Just as sure as the Son of God ascended from Galilee's shore to go back to be with the Father after His resurrection, so we will ascend with Him in the clouds when the Saviour comes back for His own.

It will be a *HAPPY* trip. How happy the glad reunion when a child of God is reunited with saved loved ones who have gone on before! One of the problems with space travel, we're told, is loneliness. For many of the men locked up in those space capsules day in and day out, loneliness was a major problem indeed. But there will be no loneliness ever again for the child of God when the Saviour comes back for our trip into outer space.

It will be a *REWARDING* trip. Revelation 22:12 tells us He will come with His rewards for those who have faithfully served Him down here.

The time of my trip into outer space is unknown. Jesus said no man can know the day or the hour when He will return for us. You will not have to be strapped in; and the scenery, you may be sure, will be gorgeous when we're caught up into His wonderful presence.

Men scoff at the glorious truth of the second coming of Christ only because they are unbelievers and scoff at God.

Job cried, "For I know that my redeemer liveth, and that he shall stand at the latter day upon the earth" (Job 19:25). Will Job be disappointed? Not on your life. Our Redeemer *does* live, and we will one day stand with Him again; for after our sojourn with Him in outer space, we will be with Him again on the earth.

Paul said in I Thessalonians 4:16,17, "For the Lord himself shall descend from heaven with a shout, with the voice of the archangel, and with the trump of God: and the dead in Christ shall rise first: Then we which are alive and remain shall be caught up together with them in the clouds, to meet the Lord in the air: and so shall we ever be with the Lord." Did Paul know what he was talking about? To ask the question is to answer it.

Jude cried, "Behold, the Lord cometh with ten thousands of his saints" (Jude 14).

John said, "Behold, he cometh with clouds; and every eye shall see him. . ." (Rev. 1:7).

Malachi said, "But unto you that fear my name shall the Sun of righteousness arise with healing in his wings; and ye shall go forth, and grow up as calves of the stall" (4:2).

Isaiah said, "For, behold, the Lord will come with fire, and with his chariots like a whirlwind. . ." (66:15).

Daniel spoke of a stone cut out of the mountain without hands in Daniel 2:45 as he described our returning Lord.

Angels announced in Acts 1:11, ". . .this same Jesus, which is taken up from you into heaven, shall so come in like manner as ye have seen him go into heaven."

Jesus Himself said, "I go to prepare a place for you. And if I go and prepare a place for you, I will come again, and receive you unto myself. . ." (John 14:2,3).

Yes, there is no question about it, Jesus is coming again; and when He does, every true believer, every blood-bought child of God will take a trip into outer space. The dead in Christ will be raised and then will be joined by living saints above the earth for a glad reunion as we are caught up to meet the Lord in the air. As we think about the trip into outer space, think with me about three "appearings."

1. THE FIRST APPEARING. This will be at the rapture, when ". . .he shall appear to your joy. . ." (Isa. 66:5). Hebrews 9:28 tells us, ". . .and unto them that look for him shall he appear the second time without sin unto salvation." Peter wrote, "And when the chief Shepherd shall appear, ye shall receive a crown of glory that fadeth not away" (I Pet. 5:4).

In I John 2:28, we are warned to abide in Him so that when the Saviour appears, we will not be ashamed before Him at His coming. This, of course, is an admonition to Christians who constitute those "caught up" when the Saviour comes for our trip into outer space.

In I John 3:2, the apostle writes, ". . .it doth not yet appear what we shall be: but we know that, when he shall appear, we shall be like him; for we shall see him as he is."

In I Peter 1:7, the Bible says, "That the trial of your faith, being much more precious than of gold that perisheth, though it be tried with fire, might be found unto praise and honour and glory at the *appearing of Jesus* Christ."

Wonderful words are found in Titus 2:13, where we discover, "Looking for that blessed hope, and the glorious *appearing* of the great God and our Saviour Jesus Christ."

Paul tells us in II Timothy 4:8 that those who *love* His *appearing* will receive a crown of righteousness, just as Paul is to receive one, when the Lord, the righteous Judge, greets us in that day.

At this first appearing, He comes to receive us unto Himself as we read in John 14, and that is the glorious thing about our trip into outer space. No wonder God calls it a blessed hope! The dead in Christ shall rise first and then we in Christ who are alive and remain shall be caught up with them together to meet the Lord in the air. In I Corinthians 15:51, 52, Paul writes, "Behold, I shew you a mystery; We shall not all sleep, but we shall all be changed, In a moment, in the twinkling of an eye, at the last trump: for the trumpet shall sound, and the dead shall be raised incorruptible, and we shall be changed." Grace unlimited will be our portion then as Peter reminds us in the thirteenth verse of chapter 1 of his epistle. Grace, mercy and joy such as we have never known before.

Scoffers, of course, will be dumbfounded when He appears to catch His bride away. They will not see Him come for us, but they will know that something catastrophic has happened. Had they not been saying, "Where is the promise of his coming? for since the fathers fell asleep, all things continue as they were from the beginning of the creation" (II Pet. 3:4)? Many religious skeptics and other worldlings today are like the Jews were at His first coming—their hearts have been hardened and they refuse to believe God's Word.

Today people ignore the Lord and cry "peace and safety," as the Bible tells us in I Thessalonians 5:3; but when men are talking most about peace and safety, "then sudden destruction cometh upon them, as travail upon a woman with child; and they shall not escape." Men will be in agony in that awful day when they realize they are left behind after the true church (saved people) has been caught up to meet the heavenly Bridegroom for our trip into outer space.

Jesus said in Matthew 24, as in other parts of the Bible, "one shall be taken, and the other left!" Indeed, thus shall it be. Saved people will have been raptured or caught away to meet the Lord in the air, leaving unsaved people behind to face the agony and anguish of the Great Tribulation.

2. THE DISAPPEARING. "Caught up to meet the Lord in the air." Yes, suddenly, there will be a great disappearing as multitudes will have been suddenly caught away in the twinkling of an eye. First Thessalonians 4:17 says we will be caught up "together." Now, what do you suppose that word "together" means? I believe that God means exactly what He says—saved people will suddenly be reunited with loved ones who have gone on before. In the Old Testament, it was frequently said that dying saints were "gathered to their fathers." What a reunion when Jesus returns! No wonder chapter 4 of I Thessalonians concludes with, "Wherefore, comfort one another with these words." There is no comfort for a believer like the comfort of the second coming.

Colossians 3:4 reads, "When Christ, who is our life, shall appear, then shall ye also appear with him in glory." How simple, and yet how wonderful: He appears, and we appear with Him. Thus we will have *dis*appeared from this old sin-cursed earth.

In Matthew 13, the true church (saved people) is referred to as a pearl of great price. Christ will come "as a thief." Thus, He will steal away the pearl of great price from this old sin-sodden world.

As those in the ark of Noah disappeared above the highest mountains, borne up by the floodwaters, so those of us who are saved will disappear above the highest mountains, yea, even above the atmospheric and planetary heavens, into the presence of God, when Christ returns.

We will go to the place of "many mansions" referred to by Christ in John 14:2.

The earth groans now, in fact, ". . .the whole creation groaneth

and travaileth in pain together until now" (Rom. 8:22). But
these are just the "beginning o sorrows" (Mark 13:8). For the
earth will go into the horrible throes and birth pangs of a new
world during the tribulation after the church disappears from the
earth's scene. There will be terrible earthquakes; the sun will
turn black, and the moon will be like blood; the heavens will be
rolled together as a scroll, and stars will fall like figs from a fig
tree shaking in the wind. Hail and fire will be mingled with blood
(Rev. 8:7); a third part of all trees will be burned up; mountains
will be cast into the sea, and the terrible calamities described in
Revelation 6 and 8 are but the beginning of God's judgment upon
the world for its sins.

This will be "the time of Jacob's trouble," as God deals with
Israel in a different way. Israel has been on the side track during
the dispensation of grace (the church age); but out of the birth
pangs of tribulation time, the new age of the millennium will be
born.

Meanwhile, above, our redemption will be complete. This vile
body of our humiliation will have been fashioned anew like unto
His glorious body (Phil. 3:21).

We will all appear before the judgment seat of Christ (II Cor.
5:10). Having *dis*appeared from this earth, we will *appear* there,
to be judged according to our works.

> A shout! A trumpet note!
> A glorious presence in the azure sky!
> A gasp! A thrill of joy!
> And we'll be with Him in the twinkling
>   of an eye.
>
> A glance; An upward look, caught up to
>   be with Christ forevermore;
> The dead alive,
> The living glorified,
> Fulfilled are all His promises that
>   came before!
>
> His face! His joy supreme!
> Our souls find rapture only at His feet!
> Blameless! Without a spot!
> We enter into Heaven's joy complete!
>
> —Anne Catherine White.

3. THE RE-APPEARING. Yes, here is the apex and the climax of it all. He will *re*-appear in power and great glory. He will come back to set things right.

"He that sitteth in the heavens shall laugh: the Lord shall have them in derision."—Ps. 2:4.

Jude 14 and 15:

"Behold, the Lord cometh with ten thousands of his saints, To execute judgment upon all, and to convince all that are ungodly among them of all their ungodly deeds which they have ungodly committed, and of all their hard speeches which ungodly sinners have spoken against him."

Isaiah 66:15,16:

"For, behold, the Lord will come with fire, and with his chariots like a whirlwind, to render his anger with fury, and his rebuke with flames of fire. For by fire and by his sword will the Lord plead with all flesh: and the slain of the Lord shall be many."

"And then shall appear the sign of the Son of man in heaven: and then shall all the tribes of the earth mourn, and they shall see the Son of man coming in the clouds of heaven with power and great glory."—Matt. 24:30.

Genesis 3:15 will have been fulfilled as the head of that old serpent, the Devil, will be crushed by the returning, sovereign Saviour.

"And I saw heaven opened, and behold a white horse; and he that sat upon him was called Faithful and True, and in righteousness he doth judge and make war. His eyes were as a flame of fire, and on his head were many crowns; and he had a name written, that no man knew, but he himself. And he was clothed with a vesture dipped in blood: and his name is called The Word of God."—Rev. 19:11-13.

Here, then, is the re-appearing of the Saviour, coming all the way down to the earth to consummate the Battle of Armageddon and to establish his kingdom.

Yes, "Jesus shall reign where e'er the sun doth his successive journeys run."

Micah tells us that men in that day will beat their swords into plowshares and their spears into pruning hooks; that nation will not lift up sword against nation again, neither shall they learn war anymore. Isaiah had prophesied in centuries gone by that one day the government would be upon the shoulder of this Prince of Peace, the virgin-born Saviour who came first to die and then to rule and reign. This is Daniel's "stone" cut out of the mountains without hands, returning to crush the wicked, rebellious nations of this world and to rule in power. Habakkuk declared, "For the earth shall be filled with the knowledge of the glory of the Lord, as the waters cover the sea."

Yes, He shall re-appear! "Shall not the Judge of all the earth do *right*?" You may be sure that God will set things right.

Meanwhile, remember, the time is short. Our life here is but a vapor that appears for a little time and vanishes away, James reminds us. Paul wrote, "The night is far spent, the day is at hand: let us therefore cast off the works of darkness, and let us put on the armour of light" (Rom. 13:12).

Two warning lights are flashing. First to the *Christian*. God reminds us in Revelation 16:15 in view of the second coming, that the Christian should watch and keep his garments, "lest he walk naked, and they see his shame." Obviously, then, the child of God is to be properly clad, both physically and spiritually, that we will not bring shame to the cause of Christ or to our own testimony. "For yet a little while, and he that shall come will come, and will not tarry" (Heb. 10:37). John reminds us, "And now, little children, abide in him; that, when he shall appear, we may have confidence, and not be ashamed before him at his coming." So it does matter how a Christian lives; and we are to be unashamed, both before God and before our fellowman, as we live and labor here for the Lord in view of the second coming.

Only one life 'twill soon be past,
Only what's done for Christ will last.

Yes, we must all appear before the judgment seat of Christ,

and your rewards in Heaven will be measured by your faithfulness to Christ down here since you were saved.

The second warning light is flashing for the *sinner*. When Jesus used the flood of Noah as a picture of end-time judgment, he declares that the unbelievers near the ark "knew not until the flood came, and took them all away. . ." (Matt. 24:39).

Think of it, the wealthy and the poor, the learned and the illiterate, the religious and the scoffers, the young and the elderly, the self-righteous and the self-indulgent, the hesitant and the procrastinator—the flood came and took them all away! Those who made excuses and those who were depending upon their feelings, along with the careless pleasure-seeker and the tired, overworked laborer, all who were unbelievers were swept away in the terrible flood and left behind when the true believers were caught up in the ark, above the flood-drenched earth. So shall it be when Jesus comes again. Only the true believers, real born-again Christians, will be caught up, for they are in Christ (the ark of safety) and will be eternally saved. All of the rest will be swept away in the floodtide of God's divine wrath.

"For what shall it profit a man, if he shall gain the whole world, and lose his own soul?"—Mark 8:36.

Let us close with the words of the Saviour in Mark 13:37, "And what I say unto you I say unto all, Watch."

Are you watching for His return?

CHAPTER 3

What Will Happen at the Rapture?

". . .he was not; for God took him."—Gen. 5:24.

A trip into outer space is nothing new. Enoch walked with God and was not found, for God took him, the Bible says. And the Scripture assures us in Hebrews 11:5 that "Enoch was translated that he should not see death." Enoch took a trip into outer space. He walked with God; and one day God said, "Enoch, why don't you go Home with Me?" So, Enoch went to spend the day with the Lord; but he never came back, for there is "no night there."

Elijah took a trip into outer space when God sent a chariot of fire down to rapture him in II Kings 2.

Jesus took a trip into outer space, as we discover in Acts 1, when He ascended back to be with the Father forty days after the resurrection.

While the word "rapture" does not appear in the Bible, the truth of such a "rapturing away" of the church is certainly evident on many pages. The launch time is a mystery; for in Matthew 24:44 Jesus said, ". . .in such an hour as ye think not the Son of man cometh."

Astronauts have to wait for good weather; but Jesus will come for His bride at the appointed time, no matter how stormy it may be down here.

Elijah had to have a vehicle for travel. We will simply be "caught up together" (I Thess. 4:17).

Visibility might be a problem for earthlings who attempt a

space walk; but Jesus, God the Son, can see through anything, day or night!

An astronaut has to have a standby as a possible substitute in case illness or some other emergency prevents his going at the last minute. A Christian can have no "standby" waiting in the wings. Every individual must believe for himself; and he will be caught up as an individual, though with the whole body of Christ, when the Saviour returns.

Space travel is exciting, as those who have followed the astronauts declare. But no excitement can match that of the blood-bought believer who experiences the thrilling rapture when Christ comes back for us.

For astronauts to launch into space, there is conceivably great danger. However, when Jesus comes for His own, the only danger will be for you not to be ready for His return.

Mere earth men who travel into outer space as astronauts may experience disappointment with what they see and behold, but there will be no disappointment for the child of God when Jesus takes us unto Himself in that glad day!

Without a doubt, the Saviour is coming as the heavenly Bridegroom to take His waiting bride away for a heavenly honeymoon. This first phase of the second coming of Christ is set forth in type, symbol, parable, arrangement, direct declaration and scenic illustration throughout the Word of God.

We see the truth illustrated in Enoch and Elijah; but also in Noah, Joseph, Abraham, Isaac, and others.

Noah, and those who believed, were caught up above the devastation of the Flood and were safe in the ark, while those who had rejected his invitation remained outside to perish in the flood waters. They suffered judgment because they had neglected to come into the ark. Even so, when Jesus comes, only those who have received the Saviour and have accepted His divine invitation will be caught up above the terrible flood of divine judgment that will devastate this world.

Joseph is a beautiful type of Christ in many ways. Joseph was rejected by his brethren; later, he was placed in the pit (as if to die there), though he was sold into Egypt. Down in Egypt—a type of this world—he took unto himself a Gentile bride and was exalted as the Prime Minister of the land of Egypt. Then one day his brethren had to acknowledge him. The analogy is clear: Christ, rejected by His brethren, is now taking unto Himself a bride (the church) and will one day later appear as King of kings and Lord of lords.

The coming of Jesus for His own is a blessed hope for the believer. The rapture is called "that blessed hope," in Titus 2:13, because

I. HE IS COMING TO RECEIVE US

In John 14 Jesus said, "If I go. . .I will come again, and receive you unto myself." In I Thessalonians 4:16,17 the truth is reiterated.

As a giant magnet sometimes swings down over the steel mill yard, picking up the true steel but leaving behind the wood, the rubbish, the debris, just so one day our heavenly Magnet, the divine Saviour, the sovereign Son of God, will swing down over this old sin-cursed earth at the appointed time; and the true steel—born-again believers (not just church members!)—will be caught up to meet the Lord in the air, and so shall we ever be with the Lord. Those who have not been saved will be left behind.

II. HE IS COMING TO RE-AWAKEN THE DEAD IN CHRIST

First Corinthians 15 assures us that this mortal body must put on immortality and this corruptible body shall put on incorruption (vs. 54).

See the truth also in Isaiah 26:19 where the prophet cries, "Thy dead men shall live, together with my dead body shall they arise. Awake and sing, ye that dwell in dust: for thy dew is as the dew of herbs, and the earth shall cast out the dead."

Note, then, that God says in verse 20, "Come, my people, enter thou into thy chambers, and shut thy doors about thee: hide thyself as it were for a little moment, until the indignation be overpast."

Thus we see the Saviour taking His bride out of the calamity and catastrophe of divine judgment until the indignation or tribulation is passed.

III. HE IS COMING TO RE-UNITE US

First Thessalonians 4:16 tells us we will be caught up "together" to meet the Lord in the air. What do you suppose God means by that word "together"? I believe that He means exactly what He says. People are always asking preachers, "Will we know one another in Heaven?" Well, certainly we aren't going to have less sense up there than we have down here—and we know one another in this life. First Corinthians 13 assures us that "now we see through a glass, darkly; but then face to face: now I know in part; but then shall I know even as also I am known" (vs. 12).

I have a sister named Mary Louise, but I have never seen that sister! She died as a baby girl just before I was born. I will have a personal introduction to my own sister at the rapture when Jesus returns and we're caught up *together* to meet the Lord in the air.

When I was seven years old, my godly mother died in Knoxville, Tennessee. I have a picture of her and she was very beautiful. My daddy came in one morning from the hospital and sat down on the floor beside me where I was trying to get the knots out of my shoestrings from the night before. When he took my shoes in his hands, I knew something was wrong because he never bothered with my shoestring knots.

He said, "Hugh boy, your mother is dead—she's gone to Heaven!"

My sun went down at midday as I sat in that lonely Tennessee cemetery and saw them lower the body of my mother into that open grave. I may be preaching today partly because of her prayers. I missed her through the years.

I've lost track of that cemetery. The city has grown up around it. But one thing for sure, God knows where the graveyard is; and one day there will be a commotion in a Tennessee cemetery when Jesus returns. The dead in Christ shall rise first. In a glorified body, made new and completely perfect, she will be raised, then the Bible says I will be caught up together with her to meet the Lord in the air. What a reunion!

How glorious that Christians never have to say goodbye for the last time! We always have something to look forward to. No wonder God says in I Thessalonians 4:18, "Wherefore comfort one another with these words." Yes, some golden daybreak Jesus will come.

IV. HE IS COMING TO REDEEM US

Our redemption draweth nigh, the Scripture reveals. Romans 8:22,23 informs us that "the whole creation groaneth and travaileth in pain together until now. . . .waiting for the adoption, to wit, the redemption of our body."

In Romans 13:11, the Scripture tells us that now our salvation is nearer than when we believed. What could Paul possibly have meant by that? Did he not know for sure that he was saved? If there ever was any man who knew beyond all doubt that he was saved and on the way to Heaven, it was Paul; yet he said, ". . .now is our salvation nearer than when we believed." But, you see, our redemption is not yet complete.

I'm wearing glasses at this very moment. Now you may wear yours because they go with your outfit or because they keep the dust out of your eyes. But I wear my glasses because I want to see! The fact that you wear glasses or have fillings in your teeth or take an aspirin tablet for a headache or have an appointment with the doctor for an operation, does not mean that you are not saved. It may simply mean that you are a saved person walking around in an unredeemed body.

God never promised that He would give you a brand new body the moment you accepted Christ as your Saviour. That comes along a bit later. "Behold, I shew you a mystery; We shall not all sleep, but we shall all be changed, In a moment, in the twinkling of an eye, at the last trump: for the trumpet shall sound, and the dead shall be raised incorruptible, and we shall be changed" (I Cor. 15:51,52). That will be a glorious reality when Jesus comes back and all of the saints receive a redeemed body. It will be recognizable and will bear the present characteristics and features; but it will be a perfect body—no longer subject to death, sickness, pain or aging.

When I was a young boy, not quite a teenager, I learned something about the art of self-defense. My daddy moved a lot. In fact, I went to twenty-six different schools before I ever graduated from high school. My dad was not a preacher, but he just liked to move. Someone would offer him a little more to work for another company, and down the road to the next town he would go. I guess he had some gypsy in him, and that may be one reason why I am a traveling evangelist today.

I don't know how it is today; but in those days, the big boys on school campuses were really roughnecks. It seemed that all of the older fellows felt that their solemn duty was to initiate the newcomers. I was everlastingly a newcomer, and I got tired of getting beat up on. Someone showed me some Charles Atlas exercises, and I began to take those exercises. When I saw pictures of Charles Atlas in the papers with his bulging biceps and his herculean physique, I said, "I'm going to get me a body like that."

I began to skip rope like the prize fighters do. I think I was one of the original joggers, jogging before breakfast. I would do push-ups until I couldn't push up anymore and chin the bar until I dropped from exhaustion. I punched a punching bag until I was almost punch drunk, but I still didn't look like Charles Atlas. I did improve a little bit, and I got to where I could keep the flies off me in a good fight, but I never did look like Charles Atlas!

And then, just a few short years ago, Charles Atlas died. I mean you can't trust anybody anymore! Here he had assured us that if we took those exercises, we would practically have an eternal body; now he has gone on to prove otherwise. But, one thing sure, I'm going to have a new body when Jesus comes again.

V. HE'S COMING TO REWARD US

"When Christ, who is our life, shall appear, then shall ye also appear with him in glory," we are told in Colossians 3:4. When Paul came to the end of his journey in II Timothy 4:6-8, he said,

"For I am now ready to be offered, and the time of my depar-

ture is at hand. I have fought a good fight, I have finished my course, I have kept the faith; Henceforth there is laid up for me a crown of righteousness, which the Lord, the righteous judge, shall give me at that day: and not to me only, but unto all them also that love his appearing."

I used to wonder what could there be about loving the appearing of Christ, that is, just looking forward to the second coming, that would make God give plain, ordinary Christians like us the same reward that the great Apostle Paul will one day receive. And then one day I think I found the answer in I John 3:2 where God tells us, "Beloved, now are we the sons of God, and it doth not yet appear what we shall be: but we know that, when he shall appear, we shall be like him; for we shall see him as he is."

Then you will note something in verse 3 of I John 3. For there He says, "And every man that hath this hope in him purifieth himself, even as he is pure." There you have it! If I really believe that Jesus may come back at any moment, I'm not going to want to be found doing something that would dishonor Him when He returns! If I really am convinced that His appearing may be soon, I will not want to be found in a place where I would not want Him to find me when He comes again.

First John 2:28 tells us that we ought not to be ashamed before Him at His coming. So we should abide in Him and seek to please Him and enjoy our Christian service without the embarrassment and shame of doing things, saying things, or going places that we would hate to have Him find us saying and doing when He comes back the second time.

I preached every weekday morning for over thirteen years on the same radio station in a Florida city. It was an early morning broadcast; and frequently, when I would go up to the door of the radio station, the doorknob would come off in my hand. Patiently I would work to get the door open and finally walk into the studio. Every morning it was the same old thing—the desk was littered with old newspapers and Associated Press reports from the night before. The microphone was loose on the stand and was always slipping. Either they had a screw loose or the wrong size microphone for the stand. I had to sit there and hold that crazy microphone with one hand while I turned my Bible pages with the other to stay on the air. The ash tray was usually full of stinking cigarette butts. The piano was littered with books and papers and was dusty and out of tune. The glass into the control room was smeared with fingerprints.

One day, however, I walked up to the radio station door and the door opened nicely. The knob had been fixed. I walked into the studio and the desk was cleared, cleaned, and polished. The microphone had been replaced. The cigarette butts were in the garbage. The piano had been dusted, polished, and tuned. The glass into the control room was spotless. I thought, *Good night! I'm in the wrong radio station!*

But, no, when I inquired, I was told, "Paul Harvey is coming to Panama City and is going to make his nationwide broadcast of the news from that very microphone." And because a great commentator was coming to town, they cleaned up the place.

Let me tell you something: *A greater than Harvey is coming!* The Lord Jesus Christ is coming again; and if we really believe that His coming may be at any moment, we will want to clean up our lives and be ready for His sure return.

VI. HE IS COMING TO REASSURE US

Now I know that some of my readers have a little problem with one verse in the Bible. You believe it because you are a Christian; or you believe it because your Bible-believing pastor would skin you alive if you didn't believe it; yet, sometimes you have a little difficulty with Romans 8:28. It says, "And we know that all things work together for good to them that love God." We believe it because it's in the Bible, yet sometimes we have problems with it. How can *all* things really work together for good? God says, "All right, I'll prove it to you when Jesus comes again."

In I Peter 1:7, He tells us "that the trial of your faith, being much more precious than of gold that perisheth. . .might be found unto praise and honour and glory at the appearing of Jesus Christ." So even though sometimes our faith is tested by fire and we have great difficulty, these things are definitely working

together for good; and God says we will understand it better by
and by. We will know for sure just exactly why it all took place
when Jesus comes. God has a purpose in everything that He al-
lows in the life of His children.

Job said, "But he knoweth the way that I take: when he hath
tried me, I shall come forth as gold" (23:10). Truly, "the sufferings of this present time are not worthy to be compared with the
glory which shall be revealed in us," as Paul informs us in
Romans 8:18.

So, it's going to be one grand day when the Lord comes back.
Fanny Crosby expressed it so well:

> When Jesus comes to reward His servants,
>   Whether it be noon or night,
> Faithful to Him will He find us watching,
>   With our lamps all trimmed and bright?
>
> Have we been true to the trust He left us?
>   Do we seek to do our best?
> If in our hearts there is naught condemns us,
>   We shall have a glorious rest.
>
> Blessed are those whom the Lord finds watching,
>   In His glory they shall share;
> If He shall come at the dawn or midnight,
>   Will He find us watching there?
>
> Oh, can we say we are ready, brother?
>   Ready for the soul's bright home?
> Say, will He find you and me still watching,
>   Waiting, waiting when the Lord shall come?

But, sinner, you won't be there! When the roll is called up
yonder, only those who had trusted Christ as Saviour and had
thus become the sons of God will be among those caught up to
meet the Lord in the air. Jesus said, "Therefore be ye also ready:
for in such an hour as ye think not the Son of man cometh"
(Matt. 24:44). In that same chapter, Jesus said, "Then shall two
be in the field; the one shall be taken, and the other left. Two
women shall be grinding at the mill; the one shall be taken, and
the other left" (vss. 40,41).

A preacher I have read after many times tells of an experience
in Texas where he was pastor. A lady with her children sat in his

church auditorium listening to a sermon on "One shall be taken, and the other left." Her husband was at home. He never went to church and cared nothing for the Gospel. The woman was a Christian, as were her older children. They had a little four-year-old curly-headed boy, the only child in the family who had made no profession of faith. The little fellow sat by his mother and listened to that sermon on the second coming of Christ.

At the dinner table that day, the little four-year-old looked up into the face of his mother and asked, "Mommy, when Jesus comes, will we have to leave my *daddy* behind?"

The man put his knife and fork down in anger and shouted, "What's that kid talking about?" The mother informed her husband that the preacher had preached on the second coming of Christ that day and had described the fearful time when the Saviour returns and when true Christians are caught up to meet the Lord in the air, leaving unsaved people behind to face the agonies of the Great Tribulation. Then she added, "Evidently, your little son was listening better than we think he listens in church."

The man said, "If that's the kind of junk they're teaching my kids over there, they'll not go back!" He fussed and fumed and upset the whole family.

But that night, while Mother was getting her four-year-old into his night clothes, the man in the next room heard his little boy say again, "Mommy, when Jesus comes, are we going to have to leave my daddy behind?" The man cursed and slammed the door, but he did not forget what he heard.

The next morning this man, a traveling salesman, drove to a distant town in Texas, arriving there about one or two o'clock in the afternoon. He got out his sample case and went out to do business. But all of his fingers were thumbs. He was angry, nervous, irritable—it was just a bad day. He finally concluded that since it was just a bad Monday, he would get a good supper and a good night's rest and start fresh on Tuesday morning. So he went back to his hotel, got his evening meal and went to bed.

But he didn't go to sleep! He tossed and tumbled and twisted and turned; and he kept hearing a little voice in the night,

"Mommy, when Jesus comes, will we have to leave my daddy behind?" "Mommy, when Jesus comes, will we have to leave my daddy behind?" He would curse and fight the pillow, but he couldn't sleep.

About daybreak, the man got into his car and drove back to his home town, arriving about ten o'clock in the morning. He drove into the parking lot of the Baptist church where his family attended services. The pastor was in his study. The man said, "Preacher, I think I'm losing my mind."

And the pastor said, "Praise the Lord!"

The man said, "What do you mean?"

And the pastor said, "We've been praying for you a long time—sit down."

He took his Bible and showed the traveling man a few verses on the second coming of Christ. But then he said, "Man, you don't have to be afraid of the second coming. The very Saviour who is soon coming the second time came the first time for the very purpose of dying on the cross to save you from sin!" He took him down the Romans road and showed him how we are all sinners and that the wages of sin is death. He showed him the verses that teach that Christ died for our sins, that He loved us and gave Himself for us.

For the first time in his life, that man realized that it was God the Son who had died in his place. He now understood the Gospel for the first time. Down on their knees they went together; and a big, strapping salesman became a child of God.

The next Sunday night the lights went low in the Baptist church in that town after the sermon and the invitation. The light came on over the baptistry, which was over to one side, about three steps up from the auditorium floor. The pastor came down the steps into the water and right behind him was a big traveling salesman in a baptismal gown.

When that man started down the steps, people over to one side of the auditorium heard a slipping, sliding sound; and a little four-year-old curly-headed boy suddenly was down off the pew, before his startled mother realized what was happening, and was making his way, wide-eyed, up that aisle towards the baptistry.

One of the ushers started to get him, but the pastor smiled and motioned him back as if to say, *He won't hurt anything, let him alone.*

The little boy came on up those few steps and stood on his tip-toes and watched Daddy get baptized. When that big man came up dripping wet out of the water, a little boy danced for joy. And people near the front could hear him say with a sob in his voice, "Oh, goody! Now when Jesus comes, we won't have to leave my daddy behind!"

He was absolutely right. You will not have to be left behind if you receive Christ as your Saviour today.

CHAPTER 4

The H-Bomb in the Light
of the Bible

"Knowing this first, that there shall come in the last days scoffers, walking after their own lusts,

"And saying, Where is the promise of his coming? for since the fathers fell asleep, all things continue as they were from the beginning of the creation.

"For this they willingly are ignorant of, that by the word of God the heavens were of old, and the earth standing out of the water and in the water:

"Whereby the world that then was, being overflowed with water, perished:

"But the heavens and the earth, which are now, by the same word are kept in store, reserved unto fire against the day of judgment and perdition of ungodly men.

"But, beloved, be not ignorant of this one thing, that one day is with the Lord as a thousand years, and a thousand years as one day.

'The Lord is not slack concerning his promise, as some men count slackness; but is longsuffering to us-ward, not willing that any should perish, but that all should come to repentance.

"But the day of the Lord will come as a thief in the night; in the which the heavens shall pass away with a great noise, and the elements shall melt with fervent heat, the earth also and the works that are therein shall be burned up.

"Seeing then that all these things shall be dissolved, what manner of persons ought ye to be in all holy conversation and godliness,

"Looking for and hasting unto the coming of the day of God, wherein the heavens being on fire shall be dissolved, and the elements shall melt with fervent heat?

"Nevertheless we, according to his promise, look for new heavens and a new earth, wherein dwelleth righteousness."—II Pet. 3:1-13.

"And the fourth angel poured out his vial upon the sun; and power was given unto him to scorch men with fire. And men were scorched with great heat, and blasphemed the name of God, which hath power over these plagues: and they repented not to give him glory."—Rev. 16:8,9.

Paul wrote to Timothy, "In the last days perilous times shall come." Jesus said there would be wars and rumors of wars, and we are reminded that men's hearts would be failing them for fear and for looking after those things that would be "coming on the earth" (II Tim. 3:1; Matt. 24:6, and Luke 21:26).

The last few years have brought terrifying change. Who would have believed a few short years ago that perversion and sex orgies would have become public entertainment in America? Yet it has come to pass. Who could have anticipated that multitudes of people would have become so duped spiritually that they would have embraced the Jim Jones cult, the madness of Mr. Moon, the extravagant absurdities of a Rev. Ike, the muddled mess of Mormonism, the abnormalities of Armstrongism, or the scary slavery of Scientology? Not to mention the already flourishing false prophets of Romanism, Adventism, Russellism, to name only a few of the deceptive 'isms of the day.

"Evil men and seducers shall wax worse and worse, deceiving, and being deceived," Paul had written in II Timothy 3:13, and it has proven true.

John advised that there would be "spirits of devils working miracles" during the tribulation, and we are seeing some of that even now before the rapture. Desire for great spiritual power can come from Satan (Acts 8:19-23). Jesus, in Matthew 7:22,23, declared that many would one day say that they had cast out devils and done many wonderful works. So everything that claims to be miraculous or everyone who claims to have "healing powers" is not necessarily of God—not at all! Today we see witchcraft, tongues, signs, sorceries, Satan worship, all in the name of religion and usually invoking or "using" the name of Jesus!

In addition to all of this, one of the most frightening trends is the Sodomite scourge in our land—even as it was in the days of Lot (see Gen. 19 and Luke 17:28,29). They are marching, demonstrating, screaming for their "rights" to live in a perverted and abnormal state and to be recognized as a misunderstood "minority." And they are rapidly gaining recruits from the young for their diabolical immoralities.

But perhaps even most frightening is the atomic bomb and its big sister—the H-bomb!

Nuclear war, or the possibility of it, is being discussed almost every evening on the world news. Survivalists are crying that "a great catastrophe or holocaust is coming!" Commentators are frequently using the word Armageddon. Most of them do not know their Bibles, but they are using Bible terminology.

In II Peter 3, Peter refers to "the world that then was" back in Noah's day and then proceeds to describe the heavens and the earth of today as being stored with fire, reserved against the day of judgment and perdition of ungodly men. Now how could Simon Peter, a fisherman disciple, have even known that the earth is stored with coal, oil and gas, the most combustible of elements? The answer is that he could not have known. Yet he wrote of it. And he did so because the Bible is more up-to-date than tomorrow's newspaper! The Bible is the only book men have written and then sat down and studied it to find out what they said. "Holy men of God spake as they were moved by the Holy Ghost" (II Pet. 1:21). Peter was "the pen of a ready writer," the Holy Spirit (see Ps. 24:1).

We know now that the deeper down into the earth one goes, the hotter it gets. Hot springs and volcanos tell us this. But the Bible tells us WHY the earth is stored with fire. Judgment!

Verse 10 tells us that the day of the Lord will come as a thief in the night in the which the heavens will pass away with a great noise. The Greek word "noise" there means a great detonation, a whirring crash. Next, in the same verse, he says the elements (composed of atoms) will melt. "Melt" is the word *luo,* meaning to loosen or break up. Next, "with fervent heat." This is a compound word meaning a glaring and burning heat—5,000 degrees of heat over a four square mile hot spot in Hiroshima when that first atom bomb was used for destruction and 68,000 people were suddenly blasted into eternity! These are the very words used by American reporters to describe what happened in Hiroshima and Nagasaki, Japan, when the atom bombs brought World War II to an abrupt conclusion.

In verse 12, Peter tells us that "all these things shall be dissolved." And the word "dissolved" is the very word in the English language used to describe what happened to the steel tower at Los Alamos laboratory when the first atomic test blast went off. They said the tower literally dissolved before their very eyes!

HIROSHIMA, JAPAN

I'll never forget the first magazine I purchased after Hiroshima. It was a *Science Digest* magazine with a picture of a huge, red, mushroom cloud on the front; and the title article was "The Sun, Majestic, Atomic Furnace." The scientists in that article declared that what man had learned to do partially in splitting the atom, the *sun* had been doing on a wholesale scale for ages, only instead of merely splitting the atom, the sun literally annihilated multiplied millions of atoms every day. Hence, the tremendous light and the great heat of the sun.

Scientists in those early days were crying, "We'll harness the sun!"

This is all very significant as we look at Revelation 16, which is one of the climax chapters of the Great Tribulation times yet ahead for this old, sin-cursed earth. One of the vials of wrath to be poured out in that day will be poured upon the *sun* (Rev. 16:8), and men will be scorched with great heat. As they are scorched with fire, they will still hate and blaspheme God, and they will not repent (vs. 9).

We are told that just over one hundred years ago a noted French scientist said that within a hundred years man would have unlocked the secret of the atom, the power with which the Creator runs the universe. "And when that happens," he said, "God will come down with His big bunch of keys and announce, 'It's closing time!' "

A few decades back, Sir James Jeans mounted the steps of the Mount Wilson Observatory and scanned the heavens. He declared two striking things: "The universe is expanding and will be dissolved." And, "It shall vanish away like smoke."

Now read Isaiah 51:6 as God describes last-day judgments: "Lift up your eyes to the heavens and look upon the earth beneath: for the heavens shall vanish away like smoke, and the earth shall wax old like a garment, and they that dwell therein shall die in like manner!" That is not quite all of the verse. There is a happy ending for those who know the Lord: "But my salvation shall be for ever, and my righteousness shall not be abolished." Hallelujah!

Jesus tells us in Matthew 24:21 and 22 that during the Great Tribulation, ahead for this old world, man would completely destroy himself if the Lord did not shorten the days of wrath. In other words, man would one day discover something with which he could completely wipe himself out! We know now from all that H-bomb scientists are saying that the discovery has been made. And it looks like man is bent on self-destruction as we rush madly on in the nuclear arms race.

Of course, the final destruction that Peter writes of will not be *man's* bomb but *God's* use of the power that man has tapped. But it appears that God is going to allow depraved mankind to go so far that he would just about have annihilated himself if the dear Lord did not intervene.

During World War II, I was pastoring a country church south of Tampa, Florida; and I would drive to my charge each Sunday listening to the radio messages of Dr. M. R. DeHaan of Grand Rapids, Michigan. He was preaching a series of sermons, which I still have in my files, entitled, "The World on Fire." He was using those verses you read at the beginning of this chapter from II Peter, chapter 3. He was predicting the use of atomic energy for destruction long before anyone in America except a few scientists and President Harry Truman had ever *heard* of the atom bomb. Einstein's theory had been carried into the laboratory. Truman knew he would have to be the one to make the decision as to whether to use the bomb or not. But the man on the street had no idea such a thing existed. Yet the preacher was preaching about it with great authority. How did he know? Because he was reading the Book that has God as its author!

In *Parade Magazine* recently, in your Sunday newspaper supplement, we were told that the doomsday clock is ticking on. The Stockholm International Peace Research Institute had just released its annual report on the possibilities of a nuclear war. The institute concluded: "The probability of a nuclear war is steadily increasing. . . . This is virtually inescapable given the consequences of advances in military technology and the spread of nuclear capability."

Dr. Edward Teller, who was instrumental in developing the hydrogen bomb, has called for the United States to expand its defense efforts, stating that the Soviet Union has surpassed the United States in military might.

A Harvard professor recently reminded us that two dozen countries now could make the H-bomb, and that France and Italy are helping Iraq develop one. Argentina now has the capability of making an atomic bomb, according to the chairman of their National Atomic Energy Commission. Many other nations have the bomb.

Newsweek magazine tells of Russia madly distributing its factories, building bomb shelters, having gas-mask drills for children and putting much of its industry underground. The article stated that Russia is "determined to win an all-out nuclear war."

Military experts have long conceded that a nuclear war, no

matter how limited, would result in countless deaths. But, according to the science page in *Time* magazine, scientists have now unearthed a grim new possibility—one that appears to extend the effects of any nuclear confrontation to all the peoples of the world. According to studies initiated by the U. S. Arms Control and Disarmament Agency, a series of large nuclear explosions could damage the band of ozone that protects the earth from the sun's ultraviolet radiation—which could conceivably destroy all life on earth. This is very significant in view of the fact that Revelation 16 informs us that when God pours out His wrath on this God-hating, Christ-rejecting, sin-loving world, He will use the *sun* to bring it about.

One scientist has called the H-bomb the greatest threat to the survival of the human race. Einstein said, "Control of the atomic bomb is an absurdity. What we've got to do is find some way to control man." He said before his departure from this world scene, "The human race stands in imminent danger of perishing agonizingly—those who know the most are the most gloomy about the survival of the human race."

WHAT DOES GOD SAY?

Naturally people are asking, What does the *Bible* say? Does the Word of God allow the possibility of the destruction of the human race with atomic energy or atomic bombs?

Turn to Jeremiah 25:31 and find that "A noise shall come even to the ends of the earth; for the Lord hath a controversy with the nations, he will plead with all flesh; he will give them that are wicked to the sword, saith the Lord." Some years back, the idea of any noise being loud enough to be heard around the earth was considered preposterous. But not anymore! H-bomb scientists now say that the setting off of H-bombs may well set up a chain-reaction which will carry not only the destructive force, but the noise of such an explosion around the earth!

Look at Joel, chapter 2. "Blow ye the trumpet in Zion." Remember, the Middle East is where the last great battles will be fought. "Sound an alarm in my holy mountain"—again referring to Palestine. "The day of the Lord cometh, for it is nigh at hand" (vs. 1). The terrible day of darkness and judgment is described in verse 2. Then in verse 3 God predicts a fire devouring before this air force as it finds the land lush and green before them and leaves it but a smoking and desolate wilderness after it has gone over.

Now Joel did not know the word "aeroplane"—not eight hundred years before Christ. Yet he writes of this air armada with its "noise" on the tops of the mountains. (I've personally landed at several airports that are on tops of mountains that have been sliced off. Some of these are in West Virginia, Pennsylvania and Colorado, to name a few. And the noise of a prairie fire or a forest fire does resemble the roar of a squadron of planes overhead—see verse 5).

In verse 6 he describes the faces of the people who are bombed turning black. I have clippings from reporters who described what happened in Hiroshima, Japan. On the outer fringes of the blast where the atomic bomb fell, people, they said, who had been white or yellow were turning black—their faces were gathering blackness. So verse 6 would seem to describe more of the results of atomic war.

In verses 7 and 8, as God speaks of soldiers marching without breaking rank and falling on swords without being wounded, one wonders if He is prophesying robot and computerized warfare. They can now send up a plane, fly it hundreds of miles, deliver its payload of bombs and return it to the starting place—without a pilot on board!

In Joel, chapter 3, verse 9, we see that these last battles will involve the Gentiles—not just the Jews, and that "all the men of war" will have to be included in the conflict. Verse 10 reveals that men will have to grab anything they can use to defend themselves and their families and that the "weak" (women and children) will have to say, "I am strong." The women libbers will not be crying to be "like men" in that day. Even now in China and Russia little children are being taught to handle guns and other weapons.

In verse 13, God describes a harvest of blood with human life being crushed out even as the grapes are crushed in the winepress. The reason for humanity's having to suffer so is because "their wickedness is great."

Multitudes will be brought to judgment in "the valley of decision," as we read in verse 14.

In Zephaniah 1:14, we again have reference to the day of the Lord, for while man and his death-dealing weapons will be in conflict, it is the *Lord's* wrath that will be poured out. No wonder even "the mighty man" shall cry there bitterly. What bitterness as men realize that all of this torture and suffering has been brought upon them by their sins.

Then in Zephaniah 1:15, God pictures this awful day of darkness and desolation as it leads to destruction and doom. And in verse 17 we find men bleeding at the pores—another result of atomic war.

Ironically, in verse 18 we find that their silver and gold will not be able to deliver them in the day of the Lord's wrath. Men today sell their souls for money. Booze, tobacco, drugs, pornography, gambling, rock music—the graft and greed, and blackmailing and throat-cutting—all for the love of money. And yet when they need help the most, their money will be worthless. Ezekiel tells us in Ezekiel 7:19 that your wealthy neighbors will be casting their silver in the streets and giving up their gold in that awful day of retribution. It will not be able to save them any more than the wealth of the Shah of Iran was able to give him another day of life when cancer struck him down.

The latter part of verse 19 tells us that their silver and gold will not satisfy them (it never does!) and that it is the stumbling block of their iniquity. You would be wise to be laying up some treasure *above* where neither moth nor rust can corrupt nor thieves break through and steal, as the Saviour advised in Matthew 6:20.

When the world is on fire, you're going to want God's bosom to be your pillow. "The world on *fire*"—how often the Bible mentions it.

Go back to Zephaniah, note chapter 3, verse 8. Here we learn that God has determined to "gather the nations" to pour upon them His divine indignation, "for all the earth shall be devoured with the *fire* of my jealousy." This would appear to correspond with II Peter, chapter 3: "The earth also and the works that are therein shall be burned up " (vs. 10).

The day after Hiroshima, the *New York Times* printed the 3rd chapter of II Peter on the editorial page—without editorial comment. Those editors felt that the atomic bomb was getting mighty close to what God said in this chapter.

David James Bradley, who wrote *No Place to Hide,* said, "My two boys will grow up to discover whether man has created his masterpiece or his master!"

In that day, "the ambassadors of peace shall weep bitterly," Isaiah said in Isaiah 33:7.

They are now developing the "C" Bomb which is a hydrogen bomb with an atomic bomb for a trigger and a layer of cobalt on the outside to carry the destructive force of such a monster around the world!

Most scientists and military men believe that a few well-placed H-bombs or nuclear missiles could so paralyze this country as to completely knock out all electrical power, water supplies, transportation, and telephone communications. In a matter of days, if not hours, there would be no more food if this happened.

Awesome stories have appeared in Chicago papers advising the citizens there to prepare for the worst. Diagrams were drawn to show the places most likely and least likely to be destroyed first. These military and scientific prophets of doom declare that 21 million Americans might die from the first attack with just a few strategic targets hit, or that 100 million (nearly half the country) could die in an all-out assault with nuclear missiles.

One noted physicist has stated that they (the scientists) believe we are much nearer to H-bomb warfare than the American people think and that no one will be safe within two hundred miles of where one falls. Therefore, no place in America would be safe except (temporarily safe) in a few isolated areas of the Rocky Mountains which would be the only place in America two hundred miles or more away from a large city or a strategic target.

Russian planes have been seen streaking mighty close to our country while their nuclear subs have been frequently spotted off the coasts of the U. S. near Oregon and Georgia, among other places.

SURVIVAL WITHOUT MEANING?

Dr. H. Jack Geiger, professor of community medicine at the School for Biomedical Education at the City College of New York, has stated that the few survivors of a nuclear attack on Philadelphia would "envy the dead." He says the word "medical" is a tragic irony, considering the grim outlook. He stated at a 1981 symposium at the University of Pennsylvania that we think of the recovery of Hiroshima after so many years, but that the A-bomb that fell there is like a tiny firecracker compared to the modern H-bomb. He describes the terrible fires and explosions that would set everything ablaze, of the bricks and masonry that would be flying through the air propelled by 600 mile-an-hour winds. He states that the firestorm created by such a blast could swallow an area of 250 square miles around the blast center.

"Trillions of insects would be feeding on the newly dead, spreading malaria, typhus, and other plagues," the professor continues. "The survivors must spend thirty days in a shelter, suffering bleeding, nausea, vomiting, explosive diarrhea. There might be one surviving physician for two thousand seriously injured survivors."

He paints a grim picture as he reminds us that even if that one doctor could eventually get to all of those patients, most of them would have already died without narcotics to ease their pain. But even that calculation is absurd. There would be no blood, no plasma, no drugs, no electricity. Yes, the survivors would envy the dead!

LOOKING FOR A HIDING PLACE

Meanwhile, another terrible fear has gripped many—the thought of maniacs and hijackers getting hold of the bomb. Young students have been found to diagram the bomb perfectly for term papers. A stockpile of uranium was recently found sitting, unguarded, at O'Hare Field in Chicago. Everybody thought somebody else was "minding the store." There were a lot of red faces, but the danger was there! Someone has reminded us that the recipe for Kentucky Fried Chicken and the formula for Coca-Cola are still well-kept secrets, but that you can get a book at the local bookstore or newsstand on how to make a hydrogen bomb! We're an intelligent lot, we are.

So the world looks for a hiding place. Most survival shelters built back in the late forties and fifties are now grown over and obsolete. Not many of the pleasure-seekers of the eighties want to take the matter seriously. The garages under the Loop in downtown Chicago are also rat holes when the bomb falls. There is said to be a 100-acre city 120 feet underground in London, England, as residents there prepare to go under the earth like rats.

It is no military secret that the Pentagon has been duplicated in solid rock in the Maryland mountains sixty miles west of Washington, D. C., because thinking people realize we may wake up one morning and find that Washington has been blown off the face of the earth!

In Sweden, a small representative city has been built into solid granite in case there is anyone left to start over again there after the war.

Two hundred and fifty thousand demonstrators massed in Bonn, Germany, the other day (November, 1981) to oppose the build-up of nuclear arms in Europe. But over in our country, we are barely beginning to get goose bumps about the threat. We certainly need to be prepared to retaliate as best we can, and God pity us if we're ever foolish enough to believe that the atheistic communists can be trusted to destroy their weapons, reduce their stockpiles, or stop their testing of such weapons.

One senator said we have only a "chicken-wire defense" against the H-bomb.

A scientist has cried that if we do not have a spiritual awakening we may all disappear in the dust of a nuclear explosion. We have been ripe for judgment for a long time now. Some say

America is too young to die. Lester Roloff cried, "No, we are too wicked to live!" I'm afraid he was right. Oh, for revival!

Before he died, J. Edgar Hoover said, "Our country is in deadly peril. A creeping rot of moral disintegration is eating into the very vitals of our nation." No wonder the pinks and punks hated him so. He could foresee some of what is coming to pass.

THERE *IS* A HIDING PLACE

But I have good news for you. There is *one* hiding place. It is a Man—the Man of whom Isaiah wrote when he said, "And a man shall be as a hiding place from the wind, and as a covert from the tempest; as rivers of water in a dry place, as the shadow of a great rock in a weary land" (32:2).

Christ, the God-man, is our place to hide, the One "by whom all things consist." The Saviour-God who made all things and without whom there was not anything made that was made (John 1). The One who stretched out the north over the empty place and hung the earth upon nothing (Job 26:7). He is our hiding place.

In Christ, our hiding place, there is *safety*. "The name of the Lord is a strong tower: the righteous runneth into it, and is safe" (Prov. 18:10).

In Christ, our hiding place, there is *security*. "Thou wilt keep him in perfect peace, whose mind is stayed on thee: because he trusteth in thee" (Isa. 26:3).

My wife and I lived in Tampa, Florida, in a third floor attic apartment temporarily right after Pearl Harbor had thrust us into World War II. We were waiting for a house we wanted to rent to become available. We listened one night to the ominous war news as we heard the drone of Air Force planes overhead. We were so glad those were our planes going out to McDill Field and not Japanese bombers. The news was fearful and bloody that day. Many Christians thought that perhaps that war would be the one that would witness the return of the Lord and the windup of all things as we had known it to be.

After the war news finished, in the darkness of that night, my wife said what I was thinking. "You know, Honey, if a bomb falls on this house, we'll be the first ones in the house to go to Heaven!"

Only a Christian has *that* kind of peace. The assurance that whether we live, we live unto the Lord, or whether we die, we die unto the Lord, as Paul told us in Romans 14:8, "whether we live therefore, or die, we are the Lord's."

And in Christ, our hiding place, there is *salvation.* Salvation from sin and salvation from Hell. "Neither is there salvation in any other: for there is none other name under heaven given among men, whereby we must be saved" (Acts 4:12).

Today, the Lord Jesus Christ offers you a threefold alternative:

Number One: Possible escape. God *can* take you right through the heart of a nuclear war and bring you out on the other side unscathed—as evidenced by the fact that He took care of the three Hebrew children who were thrown into a burning fiery furnace, heated seven times hotter than it had ever been before (Dan. 3); and they came out unscorched, unscarred, unseared—without even so much as the smell of smoke upon them!

The second alternative is the second coming of Christ. He may come at any moment. He said, "Be ye therefore ready also: for the Son of man cometh at an hour when ye think not" (Luke 12:40). He reminded us that when we begin to see the things happening that are taking place before our very eyes today, we are to look up and lift up our eyes because our redemption draweth nigh. He's coming!

The third alternative is: Go on and *die*—you *still* win if you're a Christian! If you are saved, you just cannot lose. "To die is gain," wrote Paul in Philippians 1:21. To be absent from the body is to be present with the Lord, the Bible assures us.

They call the H-bomb the Hell Bomb. But, as horrible as H-bomb warfare will be, it can be but a mild experience compared to *Hell,* the awful place of torment into which every man, woman and young person who rejects Jesus must most surely be cast! So flee from the wrath to come.

When Dr. John Rice was a very young man, he was assisting in a big tent crusade in a rural Texas area. Many lived around there and people went to church in those days in great numbers. A tent had been erected that seated two thousand. The choir platform would seat two hundred. A platform that will comfortably seat two hundred will stand four hundred if they are standing close together. They had week-day morning services. As many as six hundred came to those morning services, the men in their work clothes, women in their old-fashioned bonnets, and the children kicking along barefooted through the sawdust in the big tent. In the morning services, only the pastors and the songleader and the evangelist were on the platform. Only at night was the choir up there.

One morning the evangelist announced as his text, "One shall be taken, and the other left" (Matt. 24:41). He described graphically that awful day of separation when Jesus comes back and saved people are caught up to meet the Lord in the air, leaving the lost behind. A Christian wife would go Home to Heaven leaving her bewildered, but lost, husband behind.

When he came to the end of his sermon, about 11:00 a.m., he said that he was going to give a different kind of an invitation that day. He wanted all who knew they were saved to get up and come on the platform with him. They would pretend that the Lord had just come and that all saved ones had been taken away and up to be with the Lord. Slowly the people made their way forward until about four hundred were jammed together on the platform, leaving a couple of hundred unsaved or uncertain people out in the big tent congregation. There was a tense silence.

Suddenly a little lady began to weep on the platform, and she went out in the tent to get her husband. He put his songbook down and came up to the front to be saved. Then it began happening all over the tent. Little children went back to weep on their knees in the sawdust before unsaved parents, begging them to be saved. Some of them came. Conviction became so strong that some turned and fled from the tent—they couldn't stand the pressure in there.

One little man went back to get his wife. Being a stout woman, she wouldn't budge; so he reached down bodily and picked her up and came staggering up the aisle with her in his arms. Then she began to weep and say, "Put me down, Honey, I'll be saved!" From all over the tent they came.

Suddenly it had dawned on these people this thing is *real*—Jesus is coming and we are not ready!

Twelve noon came—the invitation had been going on for an hour, and they were still coming. It was one of those blessed services that only the Holy Spirit could engineer. At 12:30 they were counting the converts. At 12:45 people were coming by, laughing, crying, rejoicing with those who had found the Lord.

Brother Rice said as he stood out by the old well after one o'clock, drinking water from the well, thoroughly exhausted, he felt a tug at his shirttail and turned around. There stood a fourteen-year-old, red-headed, freckle-faced, barefooted country boy with tears trickling down his face. With a sob in his voice, he asked, "Mr. Rice, is it too late to be saved?"

"No, son," he answered, "thank God it is not too late! Jesus has not yet come. The door of mercy is still open. You can trust Him now. He *died* to save you." Down by that old well they went together, and that fourteen-year-old boy received Christ and called on the Lord for mercy. And when he did, he found God's precious hiding place.

And so may *you* find it right now. Trust Him today!

CHAPTER 5

There's Going to Be a Great Day!

". . .unto the judgment of the great day."—Jude 6b.

The Bible points constantly to a *great day*. The writers of Scripture were constantly anticipating that day.

To some people, Christmas is the greatest day of the year. This is especially true of merchants and others who make their biggest income of the entire year off of the Christmas season. July 4 is to lovers of America and Americanism a great day. Graduation day is for the student a great day. Birthdays and anniversaries are looked upon by many as great days, indeed. The wedding day or the birth of the first child—these are great days.

And, of course, to the blood-bought child of God, the day of salvation—the day that marks his transformation from death to life and from darkness to light through Christ—this truly is a great day!

There are great days in the Bible. When God said, "Let there be light," upon His original creation, it was a great day in the universe. When God saved eight souls out of the flood of Noah's day, it was a remarkably great day. When God chose the nation Israel for His object lesson nation, when Moses led God's people out of Egyptian bondage, when God gave the Ten Commandments to Israel on Mount Sinai—these were astoundingly great days.

When God used Samson to slay one thousand of His enemies with the jawbone of an ass, when little David slew the giant Goliath with a sling and a stone, when God delivered the Hebrew children from the burning fiery furnace and only the ropes that bound them were burned—these were amazingly great days.

It was a great day when Jesus came down to be born of a virgin, the Son of God deliberately becoming "son of man," that we, the sons of men, might through faith in Him become the sons of God. It was a great day when He turned water into wine, when He fed five thousand men besides women and children with a small boy's lunch, when He made the lame man walk who had been infirm for thirty-eight years. It was a great day when He opened the eyes of the man born blind, when He opened the ears of the deaf, an even greater day when He said to His dead friend in a graveyard, "Lazarus, come forth," and he that was dead came forth, after being buried four days, no questions asked, and was very much alive again!

It was a great day when Jesus, God the Son, allowed Himself to be taken and by the cruel hands of wicked men nailed to a tree for the sins of the world, when He could have with one breath swept the whole howling mob into Hell. That was a great day!

It was a great day when the grave could conceal Him no longer and, "up from the grave He arose with a mighty triumph o'er His foes." His resurrection day was surely a great day!

It was a great day when He ascended from the Mount of Olives before the startled gaze of the disciples, as He went back to the Father physically and visibly.

It was a great day when at Pentecost God kept His word and the blessed Holy Spirit came in power and three thousand souls were born again in one day.

But listen: There is a great day, yet future, about which the Bible speaks perhaps more often than any other subject, except salvation. It is the day that furnishes the theme for this book. It is a day to which the saints have looked forward out of the fires of persecution for many generations now. It is a day about which more dispute and confusion is heard than almost any other subject in Christendom.

It is the day of which Paul spoke when he said, "The night is far spent, the DAY is at hand: let us therefore cast off the works of darkness, and let us put on the armour of light" (Rom. 13:12).

It is the day of which the apostle wrote when he said, ". . .grieve not the holy Spirit of God, whereby ye are sealed unto the day of redemption" (Eph. 4:30).

This is the day of Jesus Christ to which Paul pointed when he said, "Being confident of this very thing, that he which hath begun a good work in you will perform it until the *day*. . ." (Phil. 1:6).

This is the day to which Peter alluded when he penned, "We have also a more sure word of prophecy; whereunto ye do well that ye take heed, as unto a light that shineth in a dark place, until *the day dawn,* and the day star arise in your hearts" (II Pet. 1:19).

The writer of Hebrews insists we should not forsake the assembling of ourselves together, but that we should exhort one another, "and so much the more, as ye see *the day* approaching" (Heb. 10:25).

Most familiar to our ears and eyes are these words found in II Timothy 1:12, "I know whom I have believed, and am persuaded that he is able to keep that which I have committed unto him against *that day!*"

Paul, in writing to the Thessalonians, declared, "For yourselves know perfectly that *the day* of the Lord so cometh as a thief in the night," and again in verse 4, "But ye, brethren, are not in darkness that *that day* should overtake you as a thief." He refers in I Corinthians 1:8 to the time when we "may be found blameless *in the day* of our Lord Jesus Christ." All of the above verses point, without doubt, to a DAY yet future, a day the Lord has anticipated through the centuries and a day He insists we be prepared for! There's going to be a great day.

I. A GREAT DAY OF RESURRECTION.

"The dead in Christ shall rise first."—I Thess. 4:16b.

Because He arose, we also shall rise.

This is our great hope as we stand by the grave of our departed loved ones.

"Thy dead men shall live, together with my dead body shall

they arise. Awake and sing, ye that dwell in dust: for thy dew is as the dew of herbs, and the earth shall cast out the dead."—Isa. 26:19.

"Why speak ye not a word of bringing the king back?" The people of Israel cried when they realized the devious ways of Absalom who had deceived them and then had been slain in battle. They longed for their king (David) again and cried out for the return of the king (II Sam. 19:10). It was to them almost as if their great leader had returned from the dead when once again he came to rule over them. To the Christian, our King's return will be a great resurrection day. There will be a great reunion in that day of fulfillment and joy. We have not seen the last of loved ones who have gone on before—not if they knew the Lord!

"Behold, I shew you a mystery; We shall not all sleep, but we shall all be changed, In a moment, in the twinkling of an eye, at the last trump. . . ."—I Cor. 15:51,52.

So we have the answer to Job's cry, "If a man die, shall he live again?" (Job 14:14a). This life is not the end. Christ will return and set things right. This life is surely not all. God made us never-dying souls. When the mournful procession in the funeral of President John Kennedy trudged to the graveyard, the priest was bemoaning, "Never again will we see his smiling face." Thank God, the born-again believer never has to have that kind of fear. We *know* we shall be reunited one day—we will again see the smiling faces of our very own loved ones who have preceded us to the tomb.

". . .I *know* that my redeemer liveth," rejoiced Job (19:25), and this was far back in Old Testament days before the enlightenment of the Saviour's words and the completion of Scripture. His cry was one of faith. And the just have always lived by faith. No wonder Paul said, "If in this life only we have hope in Christ, we are of all men most miserable" (I Cor. 15:19)!

Because of this coming great day of resurrection, the saints can better understand David's "precious in the sight of the Lord is the death of his saints" (Ps. 116:15). ". . .though our outward man perish, yet the inward man is renewed day by day" (II Cor. 4:16).

The ugly caterpillar folds up in his little coffin and apparently is dead and gone. But a metamorphosis takes place. And one day there is a bright day of resurrection. A beautiful butterfly emerges from that tiny silken casket. This is but a faint picture of the coming great day of resurrection.

II. A GREAT DAY OF LIBERATION

"We shall be changed. For this corruptible must put on incorruption, and this mortal must put on immortality."—I Cor. 15:52,53.

"Because the creature itself also shall be delivered from the bondage of corruption into the glorious liberty of the children of God. For we know that the whole creation groaneth and travaileth in pain together until now."—Rom. 8:21,22.

Paul, in writing to the Philippians, stated, "For our conversation is in heaven; from whence also we look for the Saviour, the Lord Jesus Christ: Who shall change our vile body, that it may be fashioned like unto his glorious body, according to the working whereby he is able even to subdue all things unto himself" (Phil. 3:20,21). New bodies for old. His coming initiates a great day of liberation!

> Oh, joy! oh, delight! Should we go without dying,
> No sickness, no sadness, no dread and no crying.
> Caught up thru the clouds with our Lord into glory,
> When Jesus receives His own.
> —H. L. Turner.

"Beloved, now are we the sons of God, and it doth not yet appear what we shall be," John wrote, "but we know that when he shall appear, we shall be like him; for we shall see him as he is." Meanwhile, "we groan, earnestly desiring to be clothed upon with our house which is from heaven" (Ior. 5:2). Yes, the day of liberation is coming.

At His return, the saints will be liberated from fear. Nevermore will we have to be afraid. Many people today are gripped by fear—fear of evil men, fear of sickness, fear of loss, fear of death.

Again, we will be liberated from lust. Down here it is the same old thing—lustful pictures, dirty words, evil situations on every hand. But in that day lust will no longer dominate. Seductive actresses who pose unclad will not be the highest paid performers; rock musicians will not be the millionaires; those who have lied and schemed and stolen will not be in control. Not in the day when "Jesus shall reign, where'er the sun doth his successive journeys run."

Liberation from dirt. No more tobacco smoke, no more pollution—physical or moral—no more filth. He that is filthy will have to be "filthy still" (Rev. 22:11) outside the city of our God.

In that day we will experience liberation from sweat and tears. "And God shall wipe away all tears from their eyes; and there shall be no more death, neither sorrow, nor crying" (Rev. 21:4). "Weeping may endure for a night," David assures us (Ps. 30:5), "but joy cometh in the morning."

Liberation from cursing will be a glad reality in that day. Sinners seem to revel in their profanity and filthy talk, thus further exhibiting their hatred for a holy God; but one day there will be no more television profanity, no more cursing and vile language, when Jesus comes and the "curse" is removed.

And no more excuses. The Christian worker in that day will experience glad liberation from the excuses he has heard during all of his earthly sojourn.

III. A GREAT DAY OF RECOGNITION

"We'll be caught up *together*," Paul informs us in I Thessalonians; and if we are reunited, will we not recognize one another? To ask the question is to answer it. We shall know as we are known in that glad day.

"So when this corruptible shall have put on incorruption, and this mortal shall have put on immortality, then shall be brought to pass the saying that is written, Death is swallowed up in victory."—I Cor. 15:54.

Recently the papers carried the story of a young man who had tried for fifteen years to find his father from whom he had been separated. Then one day he recognized his face and there was a glad reunion.

One of the sad things about the plight of the "boat people," clinging to escape boats as they flee Viet Nam, is the separation from loved ones, many of whom they will never see again. And what joy when some are finally reunited in America or on some other shore of safety. To us, many of the faces of such crying multitudes seem very much alike. How could they possibly pick out their own loved ones? But they do. And how much more gloriously true will it be that we'll know our Christian loved ones who have gone on before when we meet "where the gates swing outward never."

IV. A GREAT DAY OF CONSUMMATION

This triumphant day will be the builder's completion day. "Every man's work shall be made manifest" (I Cor. 3:13). We are His workmanship, and we work for Him not to be saved, but because we have been saved. And our work will be rewarded (see II Sam. 22:21)—you may be sure of that!

"Many mansions"? Yes, but are we not even now sending over the *material* for some of those mansions? (See I Cor. 3:10-14, and think about it!)

A little boy in hygiene class wrote that one should always wash and put on clean underwear because you never know when you're going to have a wreck! And even so the motto of the true believer should be to "be prepared" lest we be ashamed before Him at His coming.

God is keeping the records. "We must all appear before the judgment seat of Christ" (II Cor. 5:10). Every believer will be there to be rewarded or to suffer loss of rewards. Far too many sacrifice the permanent on the altar of the immediate. Life here will be consummated all too soon. Be ye therefore ready!

V. A GREAT DAY OF COMPENSATION

"The night is far spent, the day is at hand: let us therefore cast

off the works of darkness, and let us put on the armour of light."—Rom. 13:12.

The familiar story is told of the old gardener who kept the estate of a wealthy land owner. And when asked why he gave such tender and diligent care to the flowers and the shrubbery when his master had not been there in ten years, he replied, "Oh, but he may come today!" So the blood-bought believer knows that his Lord may return any day now. It may be today!

Paul realized this when he cried, "For I am now ready to be offered, and the time of my departure is at hand. I have fought a good fight, I have finished my course, I have kept the faith: Henceforth there is laid up for me a crown of righteousness, which the Lord, the righteous judge, shall give me at that day: and not to me only, but unto all them also that love his appearing" (II Tim. 4:6-8).

This will be pay day! The consummation will end in the compensation for those who have faithfully served Him. "And, behold, I come quickly; and my reward is with me, to give every man according as his work shall be" (Rev. 22:12).

"And when the chief Shepherd shall appear, ye shall receive a crown of glory that fadeth not away."—I Pet. 5:4.

Surely we cannot kill time without injuring eternity. Let us not forget the compensation day. In view of His sure return "we should live soberly, righteously, and godly, in this present world; Looking for that blessed hope, and the glorious appearing of the great God and our Saviour Jesus Christ" (Titus 2:12,13).

This grand hope is not a "blessed" one to the worldling. Those who "mind earthly things" are the enemies of the cross of Christ, according to Paul in Philippians 3. So the sweet by and by will be sweeter if we are busy for Him (and looking for Him) in the sour now and now. Pay day is coming!

VI. A GREAT WEDDING DAY

"Behold, the bridegroom cometh; go ye out to meet him"

(Matt. 25:6). And who should go forth to meet the Bridegroom? The bride, of course. So the church is getting ready for a wedding.

A worldly church member who was very much attached to the "things" of this world said to her pastor after a stirring prophetic message, "Oh, I shan't sleep a wink all night!" Her problem was that she had so many things she wanted to do that the coming of the Lord would interfere with.

But the bride who is really in love with the bridegroom wants only to be with him and to behold him and to enjoy him. The obedient and faithful Christian, then, will eagerly anticipate the coming of the heavenly Bridegroom.

> Coming to claim His chosen Bride,
> All the redeemed and purified,
> Over this whole earth scattered wide,
> What if it were today?
> —Leila N. Morris

The bride preparing for her marriage spends much time in making herself and her wardrobe as beautiful as possible. Everything must be just right. She will be immaculate, dressed in pure white, without spot or wrinkle. "But I speak concerning Christ and the church" (Eph. 5:32). So, as we anticipate His sure return, we must allow Him to sanctify and cleanse us "with the washing of water by the word. . . . That he might present it [the bride] to himself a glorious church, not having spot, or wrinkle, or any such thing; but that it should be holy and without blemish" (Eph. 5:26,27).

"Every man that hath this hope in him purifieth himself, even as he is pure."—I John 3:3.

And the trials of this life will not seem nearly so hard to endure as we think of "the home over there" and the prospects of being with Him, our heavenly Bridegroom, through all eternity. Yea, such trials are much more precious than gold that perisheth, as Peter tells us.

"For I reckon that the sufferings of this present time are not worthy to be compared with the glory which shall be revealed in us."—Rom. 8:18.

VII. A GREAT REVELATION DAY

"Behold, he cometh with clouds; and every eye shall see him. . . ."—Rev. 1:7.

"For as the lightning cometh out of the east, and shineth even unto the west; so shall also the coming of the Son of man be."—Matt. 24:27.

Christ will be revealed in that day, first to His own in blessing and joy, and later to the wicked in judgment and wrath. Christ is coming. Is it not "a sin not to sigh" for His return?

Christ will be revealed in that day, but sin will also be revealed unless that sin has been covered, in faith, by the precious blood of Christ. "Every secret thing, whether it be good, or whether it be evil" (Eccles. 12:14) will be revealed in that awesome day. Men truly reject the Bible not because it contradicts itself but because it contradicts *them.* In that day of revelation, the truth will come out and the sinner will find no place to stand.

VIII. A GREAT TRIBULATION DAY

"For then shall be great tribulation, such as was not since the beginning of the world to this time, no, nor ever shall be."—Matt. 24:21.

"For the great day of his wrath is come; and who shall be able to stand?"—Rev. 6:17.

Police in some cities in the East have recently hit upon the idea of filming the antics of drunks who are brought in to the police station after being arrested for driving under the influence. Later when they are sober, the film is shown. Even some prominent people are made to see what utter fools they made of themselves when they were boozed up.

Even so, one day the lost man and woman will view themselves in that awful day of God's wrath; and they will understand perfectly why the Christian lived a godly life, as well as see what was wrong with their own lives. "The wrath of God is revealed from heaven against all ungodliness" (Rom. 1:18).

"The Lord knoweth how to deliver the godly out of temptations, and to reserve the unjust unto the day of judgment to be punished" (II Pet. 2:9). "The heavens and the earth. . .are kept in store, reserved unto fire against the day of judgment and perdition of ungodly men" (II Pet. 3:7). So the earth will one day feel the terrible thrust of the Great Tribulation. But don't forget, the individual sinner will meet Him in wrath and tribulation also.

> Then will the Judge descend,
>   Then must the dead arise,
> And not a single soul escape
>   His all-discerning eyes.
>
> How will the sinner stand
>   The terrors of that day,
> When earth and Heaven before God's face
>   Astonished, flee away?
>
> But ere the trumpet shakes
>   The mansions of the dead,
> Hark! From the Gospel's gentle voice
>   What joyful tidings spread!
>
> Oh, sinner seek His grace,
>   Where wrath thou canst not bear;
> Flee to the shelter of His cross,
>   And find salvation there!
>   —Author unknown.

IX. A GREAT SEPARATION DAY

"One shall be taken, and the other left" (Luke 17:34). Yes, there will be a terrible day of separation when the Lord returns. It is ironical to see that many of the people who most despise the doctrine of separation for the saint down here, and who refuse Christ in order to hold onto their worldly and sensual companions, will one day experience terrifying and permanent separation from God and from all that is holy and pleasant and good.

Saved people will be caught up to meet the Lord in the air at the rapture when the Bridegroom comes for His bride. Lost people will be separated from them and left behind to face the agonies of the Great Tribulation upon the earth.

Babies will be taken from the arms of ungodly mothers. Small children, who found the Lord along our Sunday school bus routes or in Vacation Bible School, will go to Heaven, separated from lost parents forever. An unsaved husband may be looking up in terror as he realizes his wife has been raptured away. The separation will be shocking, indeed.

A preacher told an unsaved judge, "It's too bad that you and your wife are going to be separated!" The judge, astonished, cried, "What do you mean, pastor? My wife and I are not going to be separated. We've never gotten along better in our lives!" When the pastor referred the judge to the Bible verses about the eternal parting of the saved and the lost, he was able to lead the lost judge to Christ. Yes, there is a great day of separation just ahead.

"Behold, he cometh," John declared.

"Surely I come quickly," the Saviour promised (Rev. 22:20).

Will it be a day of eternal separation from God for you?

Receive Him now (John 1:12), and He will receive you unto Himself then (John 14:3). You do not have to dread that "great day."

CHAPTER 6

The Mystery of the Rapture

"Behold, I shew you a mystery." —I Cor. 15:51.

Sinners and religious worldlings take great delight in poking fun at the idea of a "rapture" of the saints. And in recent years some evangelicals have seemingly had nothing better to do than to join their ranks. Even some well-meaning fundamental writers have determined to rob the believer of the "blessed hope" of the coming of Christ to catch His waiting bride away.

In Arizona a handful of religious zealots announced that Christ was going to come on June 28, 1981, to "rapture" them to Heaven. Every so often the Devil inspires some religious group to sell all their properties, quit their jobs and move up onto a mountain somewhere to await the coming of Christ to rapture them away.

Thus does Satan set the unsaved world to laughing at Christians, and thus does he continue to confuse believers who are not well taught in the Bible.

It has often been pointed out that the word "rapture" is not even in the Word of God. This is true. But the fact of such a rapture or "catching away" of His true church is most certainly taught in the Bible. Not only in actual statement and through the very spirit of prophecy is the rapture of the saints revealed, but in type and symbol throughout the Word of God.

If you are a born-again Christian, you may very well be alive on the earth when the rapture takes place and you thus would be among those "caught up" to meet the Lord in the air. You would go to Heaven without dying! Glad thought!

Blood-bought child of God, let no one ever rob you of the golden and glorious promise of His coming to take you unto Himself. And sinner friend, it would be most terrifying for you to miss the rapture and not be ready for His sure return.

"Behold, I shew you a *mystery*" (I Cor. 15:51), Paul assures us. A mystery in Scripture is some wonderful truth unfolded and revealed that had until then been kept in reserve. The types and symbols of the Old Testament and some of the prophetic teaching of our Lord Jesus had inferred a rapture and had intimated that there would be one. But as the New Testament unfolds, we see the "mystery" made plain!

Of all the memorable scenes ever enacted on the platform of this world, the most amazing of all is soon to take place.

All creation groans in anticipation of a day of deliverance. But before the travail days of the tribulation and the blossoming days of the millennium, there must first be a day of deliverance, transformation and translation for the children of God—the rapture of the saints out of this world and into the presence of the Saviour "until the indignation be overpast" (Isa. 26:20).

The devoted Bible students who have been taught by the Spirit, the faithful saints who believe exactly what they read in Scriptures, the greatest soul winners of this century (and of all time), have been those who believed in and eagerly looked forward to the coming of Christ for His own.

Dr. Lee Roberson, pastor of the Highland Park Baptist Church of Chattanooga, founder of Tennessee Temple Schools, author, editor and pastor who has baptized multiplied thousands of converts, readily points to the glorious truth of the premillennial return of Christ as the great motivator for his monumental work. And, by the way, he learned what the Bible taught about the second coming on his knees with a King James Bible in front of him long before he knew about the notes in the Scofield Reference Bible or had ever read the various arguments, pro and con, about "pre" or "post" in the matter of prophecy.

Dr. Roberson tells about visiting a large Presbyterian church in the West where once a mighty preacher had been the pastor for thirty-three years. The church had had 3,300 members. Sometimes one hundred people would be saved in a week there. On Sunday nights people had to have tickets to get in to be assured of a seat. Crowds had thronged the church under the ministry of Dr. Mark Mathews. He had been a mighty defender of prophetic truth, a premillennialist, a man who fervently preached the rapture—the second coming of Christ.

But the custodian told Dr. Roberson that now that church has a pastor who does not preach the second coming and they do good to have 75 people there on Sunday night!

Dr. I. M. Haldeman, pastor of New York City's First Baptist Church, was a giant among preachers who also preached prophetic messages to overflow crowds on Sunday nights. He believed earnestly in the imminent rapture of the second coming. By all means, get his book, *Ten Sermons on the Second Coming.*

Look around you today at the fundamental, Bible-believing men who are really doing something for God—they are premillennial and pre-tribulational in their concept of prophecy. In other words, they all believe in an any-moment-now rapture of true believers.

But we should believe the Bible just as it is, no matter *who* does or does not believe it.

WHAT DOES GOD SAY ABOUT THE RAPTURE?

"This same Jesus. . .*shall so come* in like manner as ye have seen him go into heaven" (Acts 1:11). How did they see Him *go* into Heaven? Well, believers only saw Him go; and they saw Him go bodily, secretly, visibly, up to meet the Father. When He returns, He will likewise come back bodily, visibly (to believers), secretly to take the body of Christ (the true church—born-again believers) to meet the Father in the air.

"I go to prepare a place for you. And if I go and prepare a place for you, *I will come again,* and receive you unto myself; that where I am, there ye may be also" (John 14:2,3). So He promised to come back to take us unto Himself. What could be plainer? He was talking to His own followers in the Upper Room.

"The Lord himself shall descend from heaven with a shout, with the voice of the archangel, and with the trump of God: and the dead in Christ shall rise first: Then we which are alive and remain *shall be caught up together* with them in the clouds to meet the Lord in the air: and so shall we ever be with the Lord" (I Thess. 4:16,17). It certainly should not take a Ph.D. to figure that one out! He comes, the Lord Himself; He announces His arrival with a shout, and in a moment raises the dead in Christ first who are then joined by the living saints and all are caught up "together" to meet the Lord in the air.

The word "rapture" means to snatch or "catch away." It comes from the Latin *rapio,* a form of which is *rapus,* the root of our English words "rapt" and "rapture." So as the word "trinity" does not appear in the Bible, neither does the word "rapture" as such; but we surely believe both.

"For yet a little while, and he that shall come will come, and will not tarry" (Heb. 10:37). ". . .unto them that look for him shall he appear the second time. . ." (Heb. 9:28). Surely the saints of God, saved people, are the only ones who are looking for Him!

"He shall come to be glorified in his saints, and to be admired in all them that believe" (II Thess. 1:10). There, then, is a special aspect of the second coming that relates to the true believer; and there is, in contrast, the terrifying phase of His coming that spells the doom of the sinner.

We should live "so that ye come behind in no gift; waiting for the coming of our Lord Jesus Christ" (I Cor. 1:7).

"For they themselves shew of us what manner of entering in we had unto you, and how you turned to God from idols to serve the living and true God; And to wait for his Son from heaven. . ." (I Thess. 1:9,10a). Believers, then, are to be *waiting* for His return, and we are to be *watching* for His return as the Lord commands in Mark 13:37, "And what I say unto you I say unto all, Watch."

"When he shall appear, we shall be like him; for we shall see him as he is" (I John 3:2). How else could we be "like him" except by means of the transformation that Paul assures us will take place when we are raptured "in a moment, in the twinkling of an eye" (I Cor. 15:52)? Does not the Bible say that "our vile body" will be "fashioned like unto His glorious body" when He comes from Heaven for us? (see Phil. 3:20,21).

Now, back to our text for this chapter, "Behold, I shew you a *mystery*" (I Cor. 15:51).

1. The *time* is a mystery. "But of that day and hour knoweth no man, no, not the angels of heaven, but my Father only," Christ said in Matthew 24:36.

"It is not for you to know the times or the seasons, which the Father hath put in his own power," we read in Acts 1:7. For people to set dates for the return of the Lord is foolish, if not downright wicked. ". . .ye can discern the face of the sky; but can ye not discern the signs of the times?" said Jesus in Matthew 16:3. We are not to spend our time looking for signs and events— we are to look for Him! But one could almost preach a sermon on the second coming from the headlines on the front page of a major newspaper any day now.

It is true that the final fulfillment of many of the predictions in the Bible (such as in Matt. 24) are reserved for tribulation times, but even so, coming events forecast their shadows.

Purposely, the Lord keeps the actual time of His coming to Himself so that we will be working, waiting, watching— anxiously looking for Him at any time. In so living and serving, we will not be ashamed before Him at His coming (see I John 2:28). As we think of the time of His coming, consider with me:

The departure from the faith all around us today was predicted. "Now the Spirit speaketh expressly, that in the latter times some shall depart from the faith, giving heed to seducing spirits, and doctrines of devils" (I Tim. 4:1). So we today are engulfed with all kinds of wierd, hair-raising cults and 'isms. Otherwise intelligent people by the thousands are following off after oriental mystics. People will embrace "damnable heresies, even denying the Lord that bought them and bring upon themselves swift destruction" (II Pet. 2:1). The Jim Jones catastrophe is but one of many wild and unscriptural movements today. Many are slaves to Mormonism, Romanism, Mooneyism,

Campbellism, Adventism, just to name a few of the deceptive cults of the day.

And even among those who would profess to be Protestant or evangelical, multitudes today "will not endure sound doctrine" (see II Tim. 4:3), but "they shall turn away their ears from the truth, and shall be turned unto fables" (II Tim. 4:4). So all of the "strong delusion to believe a lie" is not being reserved for the reign of the Antichrist (II Thess. 2:11).

The accumulation of wealth was prophesied. In James 5, the Bible describes miseries of the rich, the heaping together of treasure of a minority of people who would look with scorn upon others, the conflicts between capital and labor, the fraud and pleasure-madness of those who in the last days will live in luxurious indulgence. Today we find all around us those who would "slaughter" the innocent through drugs, liquor, pornography, gambling, rock music. Greed has led multitudes to the very depths of depravity. And never have so many people living in an affluent society put up a "howl" because of inflation and taxes (see James 5:1).

Distress of nations with perplexity was a prophecy of these last days found in Luke 21:25. It seems the more educated and "cultured" society becomes, the more violence, terrorism and bloodshed is experienced. "Nation shall rise against nation" (Matt. 24:7), was never more true than today. The nightly news shows rioting, strikes, mob hatred, anarchy, revolution all over the globe. A recent report stated that there were more than thirty points of conflict in battle (actual shooting and warfare) on the earth at one time!

Trans-oceanic television and satellite communications are new in recent years, yet those who know their Bibles realize that this will be a reality before the windup of all things (see Rev. 11:9).

Pestilences were predicted (Matt. 24:7), and I'm sure that nothing that we now know of can possibly compare to the terrible plagues of the book of Revelation (yet future during the Tribulation), but even recently California was under the threat of a massive federal quarantine because of an outbreak of the Mediterranean fruit fly. Other states and counties battle the Japanese bee-tle, while farmers everywhere stay constantly embroiled with the environmentalists about the necessity of spraying chemicals to save their crops from destruction. In addition to this, there are the multiplied viruses and the constant fear of cancer-causing in-gredients in the air.

Palestine and the conflicts in the Middle East remind us that the coming of the Lord may be near at hand. It is no accident that all roads now seem to lead to Israel, that no newscast es-capes the turmoil in "the land" of Bible prophecy. The Jew re-mains the great enigma to the nations. All of these things seem to cry, "Be ye also ready. . .the Son of man cometh" (Matt. 24:44)!

2. The *transfer* is a mystery (I Cor. 15:50). "Now this I say, brethren, that flesh and blood cannot inherit the kingdom of God; neither doth corruption inherit incorruption."

As the soul had to be born anew in order to inherit eternal life, so the body has to experience a transformation in order to be transferred into Glory. "This vile body" could not go to Heaven as it is. We are now the sons of God, as John tells us in the 3rd chapter of his epistle, and we cannot even begin to imagine "what we shall be," but we do have the promise that we shall be *like Him* for we shall see Him as He is. So there surely has to be a transformation for the transfer upward.

We could not *endure* Heaven, much less enjoy it, without this change. *How* we shall be changed remains a puzzle, but God promised that it would be a mystery, so we need not be surprised.

3. The *transportation* is a mystery. "We shall all be changed, In a moment" (I Cor. 15:51,52). We shall not all sleep, Paul assures us here in verse 51. Many believers will be alive on earth when Jesus comes and will be caught up to meet the Lord—without dying! Multitudes of Christians now living may never die. What an exciting possibility. "Caught up" alive!

Enoch walked with God, and God took him on Home. The Bi-ble simply says that "he was not." Elijah went to Heaven in a chariot of fire. Jesus ascended bodily. But *our* "transportation" upward is a mystery, indeed. How will the Lord accomplish this?

Well, He said it was a mystery, and I'm willing to let Him surprise me. Outer space, here we come—clear into the third heaven!

He will come "as a thief." Stealthily, He will catch away the prize jewel, the church, the pearl of great price, purchased by the infinite cost of His own precious blood.

Noah's family had to be "caught up" in the ark above the flood waters while the wicked unbelievers were left behind in the raging storm. Lot, a just man, had to be "caught up" out of Sodom before God could bring the judgment fire of His wrath upon that perverted city. Noah and Lot (righteous men) were the salt that preserved those generations of the past. When they were removed, judgment could come; but not *until* they were taken up and out! Even so, Christ will come and catch away the righteous (every saved person), and then the wrath of God will begin to be poured out in the form of the Great Tribulation. "Ye are the salt of the earth," Jesus said to believers in Matthew 5:13.

Rebekah was chosen to be the bride of Isaac. She took the perilous and lonely journey across desert sands in anticipation of becoming his bride. One day she saw him—the groom appeared, and she was caught away into his tent to enjoy the bliss of wedded love. Even so, we the church have been chosen by Christ, the heavenly Bridegroom. The journey is oft perilous and lonely. But we anticipate the time when we shall see Him and be with Him. One day soon, we believe, the Groom will appear and we will be "caught away" forever to be with the Lord! He will come for us, though the transportation is a mystery.

4. The *tune* is a mystery. "The *trumpet* shall sound" (I Cor. 15:52). He shall come with the trump of God, Paul advised in I Thessalonians 4. What a trumpet sound that will be! What a tune! Celestial, amazing, glorious!

This will be an angelic blast.

The trumpeter will have been given leave of absence from the heavenly orchestra to make this flying trip to announce the rapture. A beautiful tune, surely.

It will be a commanding tune. "The dead shall be raised." Not every trumpet blast will do that! Of course, it is not the trumpet but the LORD who will bring the dead up from their tenements in the ground.

It will be a convincing tune. The corruptible will put on incorruption and the mortal will put on immortality. What an amazing moment when suddenly those dead bones are clothed with celestial and eternal adornment.

5. The *theme* is a mystery. "Death swallowed up in victory!" The world cannot understand that. The body will experience a victory then (vs. 55) just as already the world is dumbfounded at the "victory" we possess in mind, heart and spirit (see vs. 57).

What is the theme? What does the coming of Christ really mean?

a. *It is not His coming for us at death.* He did not say He would send the undertaker. There is nothing gloomy or ghoulish about this. Just try to substitute the word "death" for "the Lord" in I Thessalonians 4:16,17, and see what you get. There are those in theological circles who say we should do that. One thing

sure—you'd have to leave off the last verse of chapter 4. There would be no "comfort" in that! He did *not* say *"frighten* one another with these words."

b. *It is not the coming of the Spirit.* He had already come at Pentecost. He comes into the life and body of the believer when one is saved. This has nothing to do with the second coming of Christ.

c. *It is not the destruction of Jerusalem.* Some have even tried to tie the second coming into the terrible devastation of Titus, the Roman emperor in 70 A.D. What a fiendish stretch of the imagination!

The coming of the Saviour for His own is a personal, literal, glorious, certain and unexpected event! Only the blood-bought believer really anticipates His sure return.

It is a theme which speaks of comfort for the sorrowing, strength for the weak, relief for the distressed, faithfulness for the failing, encouragement for the depressed, purity for the sin-soiled. Hallelujah, He cometh!

So "comfort one another with *these* words."

6. The *termination* is a mystery. Look at verse 58: "There-fore. . .your labour is not in vain in the Lord."

Rewards are coming. It will be worth it all when we see Him!

"Eye hath not seen, nor ear heard, neither have entered into the heart of man, the things which God hath prepared for them that love him" (I Cor. 2:9).

When the holy city is seen coming down in Revelation 21:2, it is as "a bride adorned for her husband." Oh, what a day! The prepared bride enters the *city* that has been prepared "even as a bride." No more beautiful adornment than that.

And what a reunion! We'll never say good-bye in Glory.

> Sad hearts will gladden, all shall be bright,
> Good-bye forever to earth's dark night;
> Changed in a moment, like Him to be,
> Oh, glorious daybreak, Jesus I'll see.
> —Carl A. Blackmore.

When He comes and we're transported to His heavenly Home (and ours), we'll cry as did the Queen of Sheba when she beheld the riches, splendor and glory of King Solomon's magnificent kingdom, "Behold, the half was not told me: thy wisdom and prosperity exceedeth the fame which I heard" (I Kings 10:7).

Concerning the bounty and blessing of such riches when we come to the end of the way, it could well be stated as John said concerning the works of Jesus, ". . .if they should be written everyone, I suppose that even the world itself could not contain the books that should be written" (John 21:25).

We will exclaim with David, "I shall be *satisfied,* when I awake, with thy likeness" (Ps. 17:15)!

The wedding will take place. Are you ready? The guests and bystanders are looking *at* the wedding they attend, but the bride is looking *for* the wedding. The Bridegroom is coming for us soon. This is the blessed hope of the believer.

CHAPTER 7

Why the Church Will Miss the Tribulation

"I also will keep thee from the hour of temptation, which shall come upon all the world."—Rev. 3:10.

"God hath not appointed us to wrath. . . ."—I Thess. 5:9.

The tribulation, part of which is referred to in Scripture as "The *Great* Tribulation," will be a time of unprecedented trial, terror and judgment as God pours out His indignation upon a Christ-rejecting, God-hating, Bible-despising world.

There are three classes of people which God distinguishes in His dealings with the race—the Jew, the Gentile, and the church of God (I Cor. 10:32).

The Great Tribulation is a time of judgment when God deals with two of these classes, the Jewish people and the unsaved Gentile world. This period of time is referred to in Jeremiah 30:7 as "the time of Jacob's trouble," and in Revelation 3:10, as a time of temptation (trial and judgment) for the unsaved nations of the Gentiles.

It is true that God does allow suffering, trial and tribulation for His own dear children while they are in their earthly pilgrimage here. While He was still on earth with His disciples, Jesus said, "In the world ye shall have tribulation: but be of good cheer; I have overcome the world" (John 16:33b). In the book of Acts, Luke reminds us that the saints "must through much tribulation enter into the kingdom of God" (14:22). But this normal tribulation and testing for the believer is vastly different from *the* Great Tribulation that will be poured out in wrath upon a world that has invoked His judgment.

This tribulation time is the 70th week (seven years) of Daniel—the last "week" of Israel's national life on earth before the millennium, a week which had been postponed when the Messiah (Christ) was crucified (see Dan. 9:25). Israel has been on the side track ever since she rejected her Saviour-Messiah; and beginning with the descent of the Holy Spirit at Pentecost, the church has been on the main line in the economy of God. Since Pentecost, as the church has obeyed the Great Commission, the Lord has been taking out from the Gentile nations "a people for his name"—the church (see Acts 15:14). When the last member of the bride of Christ (the true church) is saved, the Saviour will return for this elect people, the saints will be "caught up" to meet the Lord in the air, and Israel will come back in on the main line again as God finishes His dealings with them.

At the same time, He brings the promised tribulation upon a God-hating world. The tribulation period will be the birthpangs of the new world; for after the period of seven years, He will come all the way back to the earth to establish His earthly kingdom and to rule and reign over the earth for one thousand years (the millennium) of promised peace (Rev. 19 and 20).

Chapters 6 through 19 of the book of Revelation describe in graphic detail the terrors of this tribulation time. The earth in convulsions (6:12-14); great fear (vss. 15,16); terrible fire (8:7; 16:8,9); sea catastrophes (8:8-11; 16:3,4); hideous creatures unleashed upon the earth (9:1-12); wholesale slaughter (14:14-20); the appearance of the Beast of prophecy, the man of sin (ch. 13); and the mark of the beast. Hail and fire, war, famine, earthquakes, such as the world has never seen or known before.

The whole tribulation scene will be climaxed with the Battle of Armageddon and the personal return of Christ in glory with the blood-washed armies of Heaven. Here, to finally set things right, He will break in pieces as a potter's vessel the nations of this world; and the kingdoms of this world will become the kingdom of our Lord and of His Christ (see Rev. 16:16; Ps. 2:9; Rev. 11:15).

The saints who are mentioned as on earth during the tribulation will be those who are saved because of the testimony of 144,000 Jews who will be sealed and called of God to evangelize during this period of time. Multitudes who receive Christ then will be martyred for their faith (Rev. 7:14). Those who receive the mark of the beast (Rev. 13) will thus seal their own doom and never be able to be saved.

Now there are Christians today who are worried about going through the tribulation or being slain during it. Others have been confused by teachings about a partial rapture. Many are frustrated about warped teaching that would attempt to eliminate either the tribulation or the millennium altogether, or both!

To the careful student of the Word, there are so many Bible reasons why the church cannot be here on earth during the tribulation (and thus must be raptured before it begins) that a whole book could be devoted to that subject alone! But I will limit our reasons for believing that no Christian alive when Jesus comes will miss the rapture so that we can at least get some of them into this one chapter.

Keep in mind that by the "church" we mean the body of true believers, born-again, blood-washed saints, truly converted. And we are thinking particularly of the church that will be alive on earth when Christ comes in the clouds for His own. He called it a "blessed hope" and I am sure that it is just that—a blessed or happy hope. Surely there is enough gloom and pessimism around today; and if we can find something to rejoice about, I'm all for locating it!

We are not to be "looking for the Blessed Horrible Holocaust" but for the personal return of our wonderful Lord. *The Sword of the Lord* reviewed a book that was calculated to destroy the blessed hope, do away with the rapture and have the saints of God actually desiring death so they would not have to go through the bloody tribulation. Dr. Wagner, commenting on that book, said that (according to *that* writer) we should be singing:

> Sad day, Sad day, Jesus can't come today,
> I'll live for today and anxious be;
> The beast and false prophet I soon shall see,
> Sad day, Sad day, Jesus can't come today!

Well, thank God, a true believer never has to sing a gloomy thing like that. Again and again God has told us to watch and wait expectantly for the personal return of the Lord Jesus to take unto Himself His own. "This same Jesus" (Acts 1:11) will return, He promised, "and receive you unto myself; that where I am, there ye may be also" (John 14:3).

"Watch ye therefore: for ye know not when the master of the house cometh, at even, or at midnight, or at the cockcrowing, or in the morning: Lest coming suddenly he find you sleeping. And what I say unto you I say unto all, Watch" (Mark 13:35-37).

1. Now if the Great Tribulation had to come before the rapture of the church, then there would have been no need at all for the Lord to suggest that some might be sleeping and unaware of what was taking place. If all of the terrible events of Revelation 6 to 19 were taking place, it would hardly be possible for any present-day saints (if there were any left alive) to be oblivious to them and still be "sleeping" through it all!

Christ constantly tells us to watch for His return (Mark 13:37; Luke 21:36; Matt. 24:42), assuring us that we cannot know what hour our Lord will come. He tells us to be ready, "for in such an hour as ye think not the Son of man cometh" (Matt. 24:44). God never tells us to look for the Antichrist or the terrible wrath of the tribulation, but for the coming of the blessed Son of God for His own!

2. Furthermore, it is not possible for the church to go through the tribulation because most of the church is already *in* Heaven. "We are members of his body, of his flesh, and of his bones" (Eph. 5:30), so the whole church would either have to be on earth suffering wrath (unthinkable for a redeemed saint) or in Heaven with her Lord. It is incredible to imagine that God would subject the comparatively few Christians alive at the end of the age to such terrible judgment when all of the rest of the church has escaped it.

3. We are "in Christ" and the tribulation is a time of judgment upon those who are *not* in Christ. Thus He promises the church that she will be kept *from* the hour of temptation which shall come upon all the world (Rev. 3:10). Enoch was a type of

this as he walked with God and then suddenly "was not" because God took him on Home (raptured him out of the world) before the Flood came in upon the world of the ungodly. Enoch was "translated that he should not see death; and was not found, because God had translated him" (Heb. 11:5).

4. God's people have a promise that they whose names are written in the book (Dan. 12:1) will be delivered when this great "time of trouble" comes to pass, even as Isaiah promises that God will say, "Come, my people, enter thou into thy chambers, and shut thy doors about thee: hide thyself as it were for a little moment, until the indignation be overpast. For, behold, the Lord cometh out of his place to punish the inhabitants of the earth for their iniquity; the earth also shall disclose her blood, and shall no more cover her slain" (Isaiah 26:20,21).

5. The tribulation period is "the time of Jacob's trouble" (Jer. 30:7), and the language of Revelation 6 to 19 as it relates to God's people on earth is Jewish. Thus in Revelation 7 it is a remnant out of Israel that is sealed as 144,000 Jews are chosen. These Jews will obviously win a great multitude to Christ who will be from "all nations" (thus both Jews and Gentiles), and many of these will be martyred, and thus they are said to have "come out of great tribulation" (see vss. 9-14). The two witnesses of Revelation 11 are Jewish (two olive trees); and because of the miracles they perform, they are identified as Moses and Elijah. Malachi had predicted the return of Elijah before the climax days of the Great Tribulation (Mal. 4:5). So on earth during the tribulation, we find not Christians of the church age witnessing to the saving grace of Christ, but rather we find these Jewish witnesses with fire proceeding out of their mouths to devour their enemies. This behavior is completely foreign to church instruction. In fact, the saints of the church age are nowhere to be found on earth during these days of wrath which God calls the tribulation. From Revelation 4:1 till the return of Christ in glory in Revelation 19, the church is never seen on the earth at all!

6. The tribulation period is a time of divine wrath—not human wrath. "For God hath not appointed us to wrath" (I Thess. 5:9). The church is under grace. So in all of the epistles to

the churches, never once does Paul or the other writers even mention the Great Tribulation as anything the saints have to fear. There is not one word of warning nor is any instruction given to the church to prepare for it. But Paul again and again refers to the coming of the Saviour, the day of Christ! And he calls it "a blessed hope" (Titus 2:13). We are told to "look for his son from heaven," to "love his appearing" and to "watch" for Him, but never are we warned about any tribulation or told to watch for the beast or the judgments of divine wrath! This is one of the strongest proofs that the saints will not be here.

7. There would be no point at all in a saint praying, "Even so, come, Lord Jesus" (Rev. 22:20) if we had many years of anguish and tribulation to expect before He *could* come. Nor is it likely that present-day Christians now living would even still be alive at the end of the tribulation if, indeed, they were to have to endure it.

8. Paul's Thessalonian letters prove that the saints of the church age cannot be here on earth during the tribulation. In the closing portion of chapter 4 in I Thessalonians, Paul tells us that the Lord Himself shall descend from Heaven with a shout and the "dead in Christ shall rise first: Then we which are alive and remain shall be caught up together with them in the clouds, to meet the Lord in the air. . ." and then he tells us to comfort one another with these words.

In chapter 5, he tells us that the day of the Lord will come as a thief in the night. This means He will come to take His "Pearl of great price" (the church) away suddenly and without warning and without being seen by the world. A thief does not broadcast his activities. Revelation 1:7 forecasts the return of the Lord in glory at the second advent (or revelation) when it says that "every eye shall see him." Many people get confused because they do not discern between the rapture and the revelation.

Evidently someone misunderstood Paul's instruction about the second coming in his first epistle to the Thessalonians and perhaps even forged a letter over his name to create confusion (II Thess. 2:2). So Paul clears the matter up in chapter 2 of II Thessalonians as he comforts them with the assurance that the coming of the Lord would mean "our gathering together unto him" (vs. 2). Then he proceeds in verse 3 to teach that the man of sin (the beast or Antichrist) would have to be revealed before the "day" of the Great Tribulation could come and that he was being withheld or hindered in the meantime even though the "mystery of iniquity" is already working (II Thess. 2:3-6).

However, something "now letteth" (or hindereth) and will continue to hinder the appearance of the Antichrist "until he be taken out of the way" (vs. 7). Now as long as the church (born-again Christians) are on the earth, we are the salt (preservative) of the earth and full corruption cannot come nor can the Antichrist take over because the Holy Spirit dwells within us (I Cor. 6:19). But when HE (the Spirit of God) is removed or "taken out of the way," then all Hell can break loose and the Devil will have free reign like he does not have now.

Since the Great Tribulation cannot break upon the earth until the man of sin (Antichrist) is revealed and since he cannot be revealed until the hinderer (the Holy Spirit) is taken out of the way, and since He (the Spirit) dwells within *us*, it is quite evident that the saints (the true church) will be removed or rap- before the tribulation begins!

So if we think things are bad upon the earth now, just imagine what it will be like when the salt (true believers) and the Spirit of God are removed! Then will come Satan "with all power and signs and lying wonders, And with all deceivableness of unrighteousness in them that perish; because they received not the love of the truth, that they might be saved." So the saved will have been caught away (raptured), and the unsaved will remain behind for the Great Tribulation. Meanwhile, we few despised Christians are the most important people on earth if the "powers that be" only knew it. They hate us and constantly refer to us as red-necked fundamentalists (or even funny-mentalists), but the worst cannot happen to this present civilization as long as we are here.

9. In connection with that, God had to get Lot out of Sodom before He could bring His wrath upon Sodom and destroy it (II Pet. 2:6,7). "The same day that Lot went out of Sodom it rained

fire and brimstone from heaven, and destroyed them all" (Luke 17:29). Jesus uses this illustration, with that of Noah, in connection with the return of the Lord but lets us know that He could not bring His wrath upon Sodom as long as there was a believer there. "Just Lot" had to be raptured out or caught away first! Even so, Noah and his family were safe in the ark before God could destroy the world in the judgment of the Flood. They were "caught up" in the ark above the flooded earth as those below experienced the tribulation of the deluge. "As Noah, so Christ" (Matt. 24:37-42). "One shall be taken and the other left."

10. The coming Bridegroom is the hope of the church; the coming King-Messiah, the hope of Israel. It is important to keep this in mind. Also, keep in mind that many times the prophets saw the coming of the Lord all in one picture and to them was not fully revealed *church* truth—the mystery of the rapture and other New Testament mysteries later revealed to the church. And all prophetic Scripture is not chronological. That's why you oft times find verses pointing to the first coming of Christ and the second coming of Christ all in the same verses (see Isa. 9:6,7).

In connection with that, it is also well to remember that *New* Testament prophecies are often not chronological. Many times God announces a great facet of the truth concerning His return and last things—then proceeds to turn the gem so that many beauties can be seen that help to reveal the luster of the entire jewel. This is true in Matthew 24 and in the book of Revelation particularly. But as the careful student of the Bible digs and studies (obeying II Tim. 2:15), he finds the two phases of our Lord's return appearing over and over again. First, the rapture and then later the revelation. The coming of Christ *for* His own and then later the coming of Christ *with* His own. His coming in mercy and then His coming in judgment. His coming as the Bridegroom and then later His coming as King of Israel.

At the rapture, He comes only in the clouds to utter the shout and call away (and catch away) His waiting bride. At the revelation, He comes back with the blood-washed armies of Heaven. He could not bring them back with Him if He had not first come to take them away!

At the rapture, the church age ends and the body of Christ is taken out of the world. At the revelation, the Millennial Kingdom is begun. The rapture may occur at any moment. The revelation cannot take place until the end of the tribulation. The church is one body. Tribulation saints are in two bodies—Jews and Gentiles. After Revelation 4:1, we find Israeli and Gentile armies upon the earth; but never do we find the church here. And where would the believers be with whom He will reign during the millennium if they were all "caught away" *just before* the millennium? There has to be a previous rapture for the Scripture to be fulfilled.

Revelation 4:1 begins "after this." What things has He been talking about? Church things. The letters to the representative churches. Then suddenly in 4:1 we come to the third division of God's outline in Revelation 1:19. "After this" and a door is opened in Heaven and John hears a voice as it were of a trumpet. The trumpet is associated with the rapture in both I Corinthians 15 and I Thessalonians 4. And the Lord says, "Come up hither." We will be "caught up" when the trumpet sounds and the Lord calls us. "And I will shew thee things which must be hereafter" (Rev. 4:1b). From then on, John sees the church in Heaven but not on earth again until the personal return of the Lord in glory in Revelation 19.

11. God never tells us to wait for and look for the man of sin or the Great Tribulation. He always tells us to wait for His Son from Heaven. The tribulation is not for the perfecting of the believers—it has nothing to do with the church. One man who had been talked into giving up the blessed hope told a Bible teacher, "I confidently expect to be martyred under the reign of the Beast." And he called *that* a blessed hope?

Surely it would be much better for a Christian now living to die with cancer or to be killed by a drunken driver than to remain alive until the Great Tribulation, only to be tortured under the wrath of those days and probably be martyred in a horrible fashion under the reign of the Beast. Yet God always points us eagerly to the blessed hope of the Lord's return. It has been the hope of countless believers that Jesus would come in their generation so that they could avoid death.

Dr. William R. Newell, prince of expositors and author of the hymn, "At Calvary," states, while discussing those who talk about the church going through the tribulation:

> They don't realize the absoluteness of God's grace. I say that kindly, but I say it with all the emphasis of my soul. I can't teach anything else and be true to the Gospel of the grace of God. The constant use of such words as "look for his appearing," "wait for God's Son," "love his appearing," in the epistles shows how the Spirit kept this hope alive in the hearts of God's saints. It was the expectation of the actual appearing of the Lord Jesus Christ.

And what a discouraging prospect for the soul winner if, instead of urging his sinner friend to become a child of God and look forward to soon getting out of this mess, he had to tell him to get saved and look forward to torture, misery, suffering and death under the Antichrist! It is significant that the great soul winners, the Spirit-filled evangelists, the most successful missionaries and the most effective soul-winning churches are those who believe in the imminent, personal and pre-tribulational rapture of the saints!

Dr. Newell further reminds us that the translation of the believers, the judgment seat of Christ with each Christian receiving rewards or learning why he is not rewarded, the presentation of the bride and the Marriage Supper of the Lamb all takes *time*. And such time there would not be if the rapture were at the end of the tribulation instead of at the beginning.

Dr. Newell said a friend told him that she actually hoped to *die* so as to "depart and be with Christ" and be safe. "Legalism is at the bottom of all this post-tribulation talk," said Dr. Newell.

The great Bible teacher, Dr. M. R. DeHaan, stated, as he discussed the false teaching about the church (or some of it) having to go through the great tribulation, "The erroneous teaching is in itself a fulfillment of our Lord's warning that the last days will be characterized by deception and false doctrines concerning the return of Christ." He comments on Luke 21:36 telling us that some people will escape the tribulation. "How subtle the deception. . .to teach that the church will be in this day of the Lord, while God has promised to keep us *from* that awful, awful time of sorrow. Men will turn Heaven and earth upside down and twist and wrest and pervert the Scriptures in an effort to get themselves into a tribulation which God has already definitely promised to spare us from, and to keep us safe." Paul wrote, "Let no man deceive you by any means" (II Thess. 2:3).

12. So the saints of God *do* have a Blessed Hope! Dr. Richard DeHaan, on the Radio Bible Class, reminded us recently that the pre-tribulational rapture has been consistently supported by church history.

> It is not, as some have surmised, a rather late development in eschatology. In fact, a number of second-century church fathers were premillennial. Even though they did not possess profound understanding of the prophetic Scriptures, they agreed that the Lord Jesus Christ could come suddenly and unexpectedly.

Then he quotes Clement of Rome who wrote before A.D. 100, and Justin Martyr who died about A.D. 186, both asserting their faith in this blessed hope.

In his book on *The Church and the Great Tribulation,* Dr. Newell refers to the post-tribulationists who keep claiming that some of these great old men changed their minds "just before their death" about the rapture. But the wives of, and the books of, and the associates of such men as Dr. James H. Brookes and Dr. R. A. Torrey vigorously deny this! Then he quotes the heartfelt statements of men like John Darby, C. H. MacIntosh, C. H. Spurgeon, D. L. Moody, A. B. Simpson, I. M. Haldeman, J. Wilbur Chapman, A. J. Gordon, H. A. Ironside, and A. C. Gaebelein, all of whom were eagerly anticipating the rapture of the church.

But of course, in the final analysis the big question is: What does *God* say? And since the Bible expressly teaches that the church will be "caught away" before the tribulation rages upon this earth, we may confidently cry with John on Patmos, "Even so, come, Lord Jesus" (Rev. 22:20).

Oh, be sure today that you are in that number of the redeemed—that you have truly trusted Christ as your own personal Saviour and Lord. Then His coming will for you be, indeed, a Blessed Hope!

Chapter 8

The King Is Coming

"Who is this King of glory?"—Ps. 24:8.

"Behold, he cometh. . . ."—Rev. 1:7.

The coming of the King is the theme of the last book in the Bible. In Revelation 4:2 we read, "Behold, a *throne* was set in heaven." In Revelation 15:3 Christ is called "thou king of saints." As Revelation 19:16 describes the glory of the descending Saviour, He is called "King of kings, and Lord of lords." And in Revelation 20 we read of those who shall live and *reign* with Christ a thousand years.

"Behold, he cometh!" Yes, the King is coming again.

"Behold your King" (John 19:14), Pilate said, and how right he was! The world is looking for a man to trust, to believe in, to acclaim, to crown!

From Genesis to Revelation the Bible announces such a King.

The Old Testament cried He is coming.

The Gospels declare He has come.

The Epistles and the book of Revelation announce, "He is coming again!"

In II Samuel 7:26 we have a promise that the house of David would be established forever—even in great David's greater Son.

In the second Psalm, as David describes the heathen nations "raging" and the rulers taking counsel together against the Lord, suddenly *God* breaks in and announces, "Yet have I set my *King* upon my holy hill of Zion." Later in the chapter he describes the King breaking the heathen nations with a rod of iron and dashing them in pieces like a potter's vessel (vs. 9).

So the King is coming to execute judgment!

The beautiful 24th Psalm asks the question, "Who is this King of glory? The Lord strong and mighty, the Lord mighty in battle. Lift up your heads, O ye gates; even lift them up, ye everlasting doors; and the King of glory shall come in" (vss. 8,9).

"All kings shall fall down before him: all nations shall serve him. . . . His name shall endure for ever: his name shall be continued as long as the sun: and men shall be blessed in him: all nations shall call him blessed" (Ps. 72:11,17).

Isaiah surely identifies the Saviour in chapter 9, verse 6, when he exclaims, "For unto us a child is born, unto us a son is given: and the government shall be upon his shoulder: and his name shall be called Wonderful, Counsellor, The mighty God, The everlasting Father, The Prince of Peace."

Then, "Of the increase of his government and peace there shall be no end, upon the throne of David, and upon his kingdom, to order it, and to establish it with judgment and with justice from henceforth even for ever" (Isa. 9:7).

Again in Isaiah 32 the great prophet exclaims, "Behold a king shall reign in righteousness, and princes shall rule in judgment." As you read on you have no doubt that it is King Jesus he is talking about.

Jeremiah stands back in awe as he cries, "Who would not fear thee, O King of nations? . . . But the Lord is the true God, he is the living God, and an everlasting king: at his wrath the earth shall tremble, and the nations shall not be able to abide his indignation" (Jer. 10:7,10).

Bloody King Herod was troubled about the advent of the Saviour and inquired of the wise men (Matt. 2:7,8) what time the Christmas star appeared and commanded, "Go and search dilligently for the young child; and when ye have found him, bring me word again, that I may come and worship him also." He was afraid of the one "born King of the Jews."

Angels, too, were excited about the first coming of the King. One of them said to Mary, "He shall be great, and shall be called the Son of the Highest: and the Lord God shall give unto him the throne of his father David: And he shall reign over the house of

Jacob for ever; and of his kingdom there shall be no end" (Luke 1:32,33).

The world wants a *kingdom*—but there will be no kingdom without the King. Jesus taught us to pray, "Thy kingdom come," but the Scripture is careful to reveal that men's hearts have to be changed before they could enjoy such a kingdom, and that Christ Himself must come as King of kings and Lord of lords to bring it about.

Just before the ascension of Jesus, the apostles whom He had chosen cried, "Lord, wilt thou at this time restore again the kingdom to Israel?" Jesus proceeded to inform them that it was not for them to know the times or the seasons which the Father had put in his own power, that they were to be Spirit-filled witnesses for Him in this age, and that one day He would come back, first to receive his own, and then a bit later to establish His kingdom upon the earth (Acts 1).

Paul the apostle honors "The King eternal, immortal, invisible, the only wise God" in I Timothy 1:17.

The writer of Hebrews tells us that all the angels of God worship Him (Heb. 1:6) and then declares, "But unto the Son he saith, Thy throne, O God, is for ever and ever: a sceptre of righteousness is the sceptre of thy kingdom" (Heb. 1:8).

Everything leading up to the coming of the King is climaxed in the book of Revelation where He is exalted as King of kings!

I ask you, does God promise a King?

He is the King of Israel, the King of the nations, the King of saints!

His is the right to rule!

Over the redeemed earth He shall reign for a thousand years, but over His saints "He shall reign for ever and ever"! No wonder Handel was so inspired to write this so beautifully in *The Messiah*.

Have we heard enough evidence? Is there a *King* of Heaven? Does God promise a kingdom? Will the King *come*?

Well, He came the *first* time: "But when the fullness of time was come, God sent forth his Son, made of a woman, made under the law, To redeem them that were under the law, that we might receive the adoption of sons" (Gal. 4:4,5).

How carefully God planned it all.

So far as the *race* is concerned, he was to come through Adam. But what *nation*?—"Now to *Abraham* were the promises spoken and to his seed."

Abraham was the nation and Judah was the tribe. There was divine expectancy all through the Old Testament.

The *time* is discovered in Daniel 9:25.

The *town* was disclosed by Micah 5:2.

Mary is the virgin person who would be the vessel for the arrival of the King, angels tell us in Matthew 1:20-23. Many facts were revealed to the shepherds who were told,"Ye shall find the babe wrapped in swaddling clothes, lying in a manger" (Luke 2:12).

The wise men were led to the very house where they bestowed upon Him their gifts (Matt. 2:11).

So He came the first time and He will come again.

In Genesis 3:15 the seed of the woman is prophesied as bruising the head of that old serpent the Devil, and in Romans 16:20 God tells us that it will take place when the King returns, "And the God of peace shall bruise Satan under your feet shortly."

He came the first time as a baby, virgin born, in weakness. He will come again as the Lord of battle in strength!

When He came the first time, angels came down to announce His arrival; and when He comes again, the blood-washed armies of Heaven will be with Him (Rev. 19:14).

When He came the first time, He was in subjection to His parents. When He comes the second time, He will bring all men into subjection unto Himself.

When He came the first time, He was a "tender plant." When He comes again, He will be "the Lion of the tribe of Juda" (Rev. 5:5).

When He came the first time, He had "no place to lay His head." When He comes again, He will rightfully rule as a resident of a palace and will house His own in "many mansions" (John 14:2).

When He came the first time, His enemies cried, "We will not have this man to reign over us"! When He comes again, the book of Revelation announces, "And he shall reign for ever and ever" (Rev. 11:15).

When He came the first time, He was "the stone which the builders rejected." When He comes again, He will be acknowledged as the "headstone of the corner."

When He came the first time, He gave His back to the smiters, and His cheeks to them that plucked off the hair. He hid not His face from shame and spitting (Isa. 50:6). When He comes again, the "government will be upon his shoulder, and His name shall be called Wonderful" (Isa. 9:6).

When He came the first time, He was crowned with thorns. When He comes again, He will receive the crown of the universe.

When He came the first time, He was given a throne on a gibbet of shame. When He comes again, "The kingdoms of this world are become the kingdoms of our Lord and of his Christ" (Rev. 11:15).

When He came the first time, they smote Him with their hands. When He comes the second time, men will cry for the rocks and mountains to fall on them and hide them from the face of Him that sitteth upon the throne (Rev. 6:16).

When He came the first time, the soldiers gambled for His robe and left Him on the cross in shame. When He comes the second time, He will be robed with "a vesture dipped in blood" (Rev. 19:13).

When He came the first time, "his own received him not"; but when He comes again, "all Israel shall be saved" (Rom. 11:26).

When He came the first time, men heard the cry of a tiny baby. When He comes the second time, He will "descend from heaven with a shout" (I Thess. 4:16).

When He came the first time, He was attended by a virgin mother and lowly shepherds. When He comes the second time, He shall "come with fire and with his chariots like a whirlwind, to render his anger with fury, and his rebuke with flames of fire" (Isa. 66:15).

When He came the first time, He came by process of birth and few saw Him. When He comes the second time, "Behold, he cometh with clouds; and every eye shall see him, and they also which pierced him: and all kindreds of the earth shall wail because of him" (Rev. 1:7).

When He came the first time, He came as a lowly one, peacefully. When He comes again, "The Lord Jesus shall be revealed from heaven with his mighty angels, In flaming fire taking vengeance on them that know not God, and that obey not the gospel of our Lord Jesus Christ" (II Thess. 1:7,8).

"Who *is* this King of glory? The Lord of Hosts!" He is Lord of lords, "the high and lofty one who inhabiteth eternity, whose name is Holy" (Isa. 57:15). "He is before all things, and by him all things consist" (Col. 1:17).

Isaiah 40:12 tells us that He measures the waters in the hollow of His hand and He metes out heaven with the span, and comprehends the dust of the earth in a measure, and weighs the mountains in scales, and the hills in a balance! The King is no mere man to be trifled with. He is the Lord of the universe! He "thought it not robbery to be equal with God" (Phil. 2:6), for He was God. He is "the Alpha and the Omega, the beginning and the ending" (Rev. 1:8). He has the priority in all things.

"The earth is the Lord's and the fullness thereof; the world, and they that dwell therein" (Ps. 24:1). We do not belong to ourselves; we are subject unto Him.

I. CONSIDER WHO THE KING IS

1. We are His by creation: "All things were made by him; and without him was not any thing made that was made" (John 1:3). "All things were created by him, and for him" (Col. 1:16b). Hebrews 1:2 tells us by Him God made the worlds, ". . .by whom also he made the worlds."

2. We are His by ownership: God does not have to rob your freezer when He is hungry. He declares, "I will take no bullock out of thy house, nor he goats out of thy folds. For every beast of the forest is mine, and the cattle upon a thousand hills. I know all the fowls of the mountains: and the wild beasts of the field are mine. If I were hungry, I would not tell thee: for the world is mine, and the fullness thereof" (Ps. 50:9-12).

3. We are His by redemption: Romans 8:22-23 tells us that along with God's material creation we ourselves are waiting for the redemption of our body. This is made possible only by the redemption which is sung about in Revelation 5:9. Christ redeemed us to God by His blood!

II. CONSIDER WHERE THE KING CAME FROM

1. He came from creation's throne: Christ said in his great high priestly prayer, "I came out from thee" (John 17:8). In Revelation 4:11 we find the living creatures around the throne of Heaven singing to Christ, "Thou art worthy, O Lord, to receive glory and honour and power: for thou hast created all things, and for thy pleasure they are and were created."

2. From Heaven itself: "In my Father's house are many mansions," are the beautiful words so frequently quoted from John 14:2. "The bread of God is he which cometh down from heaven" (John 6:33).

3. From the womb of a virgin: "Therefore the Lord himself shall give you a sign; Behold, a virgin shall conceive, and bear a son, and shall call his name Immanuel" (Isa. 7:14).

4. From the tomb of death: "I am he that liveth, and was dead; and, behold, I am alive for evermore, Amen; and have the keys of hell and death" (Rev. 1:18). "He has begotten us again unto a lively hope by the *resurrection* of Jesus Christ from the dead" (I Peter 1:3b).

III. CONSIDER THE REIGN OF THE KING

Imagine a king on this earth reigning by love!

1. He loved all men: "God so loved the world" (John 3:16).

2. He died for all men: "He is the propitiation for our sins; and not for ours only, but also for the sins of the whole world" (I John 2:2).

3. He is the only king who could forgive sin: Eph. 1:7 tells us, "In whom we have redemption through his blood, the forgiveness of sins, according to the riches of his grace."

4. He is the only king able to give life: "I am come that they might have life, and that they might have it more abundantly" (John 10:10).

5. He is the only king who can grant *any* request: "If ye shall ask any thing in my name, I will do it" (John 14:14).

6. He is the only king who can restore health: Many kings have died themselves or lived to see their loved ones pass into the regions of death. Christ is the King who has brought back the bloom of health to many a cheek, the strength of life to many a drooping spirit. A doctor in Michigan some time ago had worked out a diet by which he planned to live to be one hundred years old. He died at the age of ninety. Naaman, the Syrian, was a man of wealth and influence but was unable to cure the leprosy of his body—only God could prescribe the Jordanian remedy (II Kings 5).

7. He is the only king who can give peace: His very name Immanuel means "God with us." If God be for us who can be against us? He alone, then, could say, "These things I have spoken unto you, that in me ye might have peace" (John 16:33).

IV. THIS KING DIED A DEATH LIKE NO OTHER MAN

His bloody death was vicarious, atoning, substitutionary! "For Christ also hath once suffered for sins, the just for the unjust, that he might bring us to God" (I Pet. 3:18a). He was made "to be sin for us, . . . that we might be made the righteousness of God in him" (II Cor. 5:21). They said, "Never man spake like this man." They could also have said, "Never did one die like King Jesus!"

V. THE KING NOW GATHERS MEN TO REIGN WITH HIM

What kind of men? Well, Colossians 1:13 tells us He "hath delivered us from the power of *darkness,* and hath translated us into the kingdom of his dear Son." Not only were we in darkness but we were in weakness, "Yet without strength" (Rom. 5:6). "God hath chosen the weak things" (I Cor. 1:27).

What kind of men? "He gathers together the *outcasts* of Israel" (Ps. 147:2). He delights to take in Mary Magdalene or a thief on the cross and make them trophies of grace!

"While we were yet sinners, Christ died for us" (Rom. 5:6). What a variety of men He gathers: fishermen, shepherds, blind men, lepers, maniacs! Truly, "Not many wise men after the flesh, not many mighty, not many noble, are called" (I Cor. 1:26).

VI. BUT THE KING IS COMING AGAIN!

He said, 'If I go, I will come again!' (John 14:3). "This same Jesus," was Heaven's announcement. He is coming back!

"Behold, He cometh!" Acts 3 tells us that the heavens have received Him until the times of restitution of all things (vs. 21).

He is interceding for us. He is our Advocate.

But He also is our coming King!

1. Every eye shall see Him: Perhaps until television came on the scene it was difficult to imagine how every person on a round earth could witness the return of Christ at one time. Whether TV has anything to do with it or not, the Scripture will be fulfilled and every eye shall see Him when He comes again!

2. He will sit upon the throne of David: Every blessed word of Luke 1 will be fulfilled. Those angels made no mistake. "He shall be great, and shall be called the Son of the Highest: and the Lord God shall give unto him the throne of his father David" (Luke 1:32).

3. Righteousness will reign over the earth: We may witness little spurts of righteousness and decency occasionally in this world, but the only true righteousness is that provided by Christ. Our righteousness is in Him. Shovel snow down here and it snows again. Wash your hands this morning and you will wash them again at noon. In this life anything to make clean or make right has to be repeated. How good to know that righteousness will one day *reign!* "With righteousness shall he judge the poor, and reprove with equity for the meek of the earth" (Isa. 11:4).

"Righteousness shall be the girdle of his loins, and faithfulness the girdle of his reins" (Isa. 11:5). "In his days Judah shall be saved, and Israel shall dwell safely: and this is the name whereby he shall be called, THE LORD OUR RIGHTEOUSNESS" (Jer. 23:6). "In righteousness he doth judge and make war" (Rev. 19:11). The Saviour is the only King to declare war in perfect righteousness.

4. Earth's curse will be removed: Today the whole creation groans and travails in pain (Rom. 8:22). But when the King sets up His kingdom, "the wolf also shall dwell with the lamb, and the leopard shall lie down with the kid; and the calf and the young lion and the fatling together; and a little child shall lead them" (Isa. 11:6). Verses 7 and 8 describe the lion eating straw like the ox and the little tot playing with serpents. Today if the lion should lie down with the lamb you may be certain the lamb would be on the *inside!* I remember a little verse from childhood:

> "There once was a lady from Niger,
> Who smiled as she rode on a tiger;
> They came back from the ride with the lady inside;
> And the smile on the face of the tiger!"

5. God's enemies will be justly punished: "He will break them with a rod of iron" (Ps. 2:9). The Stone cut out of the mountains without hands (the eternal Rock of Ages) will descend upon the nations of this world (Dan. 2:44,45).

"The kingdoms of this world are become the kingdoms of our Lord, and of his Christ" (Rev. 11:15).

"The Lord will come with fire, and with his chariots like a whirlwind, to render his anger with fury" (Isa. 66:15).

Read the book of Revelation and you will witness the indignation of the Lord poured out upon a Christ-rejecting, God-hating world.

God's enemies must be punished. At His return He will say to them on the left hand, "Depart from me, ye cursed, into everlasting fire, prepared for the devil and his angels" (Matt. 25:41). In verse 46 of the same chapter we read of some who "go away into everlasting punishment: but the righteous into life eternal."

Surely the cup of God's indignation must be about full. As one man has put it, "I have stopped looking for signs and am listening for sounds" of his return!

Yes, the King is coming!

He is coming back to the earth, as He promised.

But *first,* He must come in the clouds for His own. Before He comes as King He must come as Bridegroom—to catch His waiting Bride away!

In that day, "One shall be taken, and the other left." Those who are saved will be caught up to meet the Lord in the air while the unsaved are left behind to face the throes and agonies of the Great Tribulation (Matt. 24:40).

"This same Jesus" will return for His own at the right time.

"I will come again and receive you unto myself," the Saviour said in the beautiful upper room discourse.

Can you not hear Him now?—"Rise up, my love, my fair one, and come away" (Song of Sol. 2:10).

This is the "come up hither" of Revelation 4:1.

In Isaiah 26:20 we find the Lord saying, "Come, my people, enter thou into thy chambers, and shut thy doors about thee: hide thyself as it were for a little moment, until the indignation be overpast." Yes, the tribulation and indignation of the Lord will be felt on the earth—but not by those who are ready for His return.

"Therefore be ye also ready: for in such an hour as ye think not the Son of man cometh" (Matt. 24:44).

One of these days every knee shall bow and every tongue shall confess that Jesus Christ is Lord to the glory of God the Father (Phil. 2:10,11). So, beloved, it is not a matter of whether or not you *will* bow before Christ and confess Him as Lord. It is just a question of *WHEN* will you do it? You can receive Him now and He can become your Lord and Saviour, or you can wait until the other side of the grave when it is everlastingly too late to be saved!

Remember, His arrows "are sharp in the heart of the king's enemies" (Ps. 45:5). Don't wait for Him to have to shoot you down!

I once was asked to assist four other preachers in conducting a funeral of a lost man. Frantically the family seemed to be grabbing at a straw. Each of the five of us read some Scripture and prayed. But all five of us together could do nothing about getting that man's soul into Heaven after his breath had left his body.

The King is coming, and death is coming!

Oh, believe and be saved today!

CHAPTER 9

The Joy of the Second Coming

"Joy cometh in the morning."—Ps. 30:5.

To know and understand the truth of His sure return will bring joy to the heart of a believer like no other doctrine or experience. It is the most practical of incentives for victorious Christian living. Truly the promise of His second coming for us, and then to set all things right, is a transforming hope—yea it is indeed *the* blessed hope (see Titus 2:13).

His coming is spoken of more often, and associated with more doctrines, and mentioned in more verses than any other theme of the Bible other than salvation itself. Such a hope Jesus expressed when He said, "And when these things begin to come to pass, then look up, and lift up your heads; for your redemption draweth nigh" (Luke 21:28).

The New Testament constantly looks forward to the second coming of the Lord. And so should we! Paul wrote, "Therefore judge nothing before the time, until the Lord come, who both will bring to light the hidden things of darkness, and will make manifest the counsels of the hearts: and then shall every man have praise of God" (I Cor. 4:5). He told the Philippians to approve things that are excellent and to be sincere and without offense *until the day* of Christ—that is, the day when the Saviour comes again (Phil. 1:10).

In Colossians 3:2-4 he declared, "Set your affection on things above, not on things on the earth. . . . When Christ, who is our life, shall appear, then shall ye also appear with him in glory."

So believers are to watch for the appearing of the Lord while we live for Him. As Jesus put it, "Blessed is that servant, whom his lord when he cometh shall find so doing" (Luke 12:43).

In writing to Titus, God (through Paul) reminds us that this wonderful grace of Jesus (Titus 2:11,12) teaches us that, "denying ungodliness and worldly lusts, we should live soberly, righteously, and godly in this present world," while looking for that blessed hope in the sure return of Jesus. A "blessed" hope is a *happy* hope. Ungodly people and people who live in worldly lusts are miserable people. They stumble out of one wretched situation into another. Their problems never cease. They're always trying to "cover up." They add sin to sin. They walk in the flesh. They serve the Devil, whether they know it or not. They are slaves to this world. Their eyes are dim to the world beyond. They have no assurance, no security; and if they are not saved, they indeed have no hope.

We do not have to look far to discover that *sober* people are happier than drunken people. They are not bound by habit; they are not slaves to sin. The grace they have to face the daily battle does not come from a bottle. Soberness also means seriousness. The obedient child of God who lives in anticipation of the Lord's return is serious about life and eternity. But he does not have to fear life, death *or* eternity. He can live life to the fullest in quiet confidence.

In view of His coming we are also enjoined to live *righteously* (Titus 2:12). Righteous people are those who have received the perfect righteousness which God gives us in Christ. We have the personal righteousness to combat life's temptations because of the indwelling Spirit of God. Righteousness also denotes righteous *acts*. People who are righteous live righteously.

And, awaiting His return, we are to live *godly* in this present world. To be godly is to be like God, to honor God, to think upon Him, to obey His Word, to have fellowship with Him. One old saint wrote of "practicing the presence of the Lord." That is what it means to be godly. This we are to be as we look for the blessed hope.

Does living soberly, righteously and godly produce JOY? It

does if we live this way in anticipation of His return—the blessed hope.

In this land of ours where, as Lester Roloff properly said, "America is one big insane asylum run by the inmates," we could use something that produces real joy. What are some of the blessed promises that produce such joy?

I. THE FIRST JOY OF THE SECOND COMING IS THE RESURRECTION OF THE DEAD IN CHRIST.

"By one man sin entered into the world, and death by sin," Paul teaches us in Romans 5:12. Hebrews teaches us that it is appointed unto man once to die. Death is sure for all people except believers who will be fortunate enough to be alive on earth when Christ comes for His own.

But our resurrected Saviour said, "I am he that liveth, and was dead; and, behold, I am alive for evermore, Amen; and have the keys of hell and of death" (Rev. 1:18). Because He lives we shall live also. Our saved loved ones who have been buried have not been heard the last of!

The creation groans, waiting for the adoption, the redemption of the body, Paul reveals in Romans 8:23.

> In the resurrection morning, When the trump of God shall sound,
>   We shall rise, Hallelujah, we shall rise!
> Then the saints will come rejoicing and no tears will e'er be found,
>   We shall rise, We shall rise.
>
> We shall rise! We shall rise, Amen! We shall rise. . .
>   In the resurrection morning, When death's prison bars are broken,
> We shall rise, Hallelujah, we shall rise!
>
> —J. E. T.

When He comes He "shall change our vile body, that it may be fashioned like unto his glorious body, according to the working whereby he is able even to subdue all things unto himself" (see Phil. 3:20,21). Yes, one of the joys of the second coming is the promised resurrection of the body. And remember, Romans 8:23 promises the redemption *of,* not deliverance *from,* the body. You will have your body in a glorified form forever!

Imagine seeing the great old men and women of God in their

bodies—they will come off the pages of your Bible and be standing there in person! Abel with no threat of murder from his brother; Noah with no ark to build to escape another flood; Abraham with no temptation to go down to Egypt; Joesph no longer despised by his brethren or tempted by Potiphar's wife; Moses no longer having to look for God in a burning bush; John the Baptist never again to be beheaded; John never more to be exiled on a lonely Patmos; and Paul minus his thorn in the flesh! Hallelujah, indeed!

II. A SECOND JOY OF THE SECOND COMING IS THE RAPTURE AND TRANSFIGURATION OF LIVING CHRISTIANS.

"We shall not all sleep, but we shall all be changed" in that glorious day of rapture and reunion. Some golden daybreak Jesus *will* come!

People say death (along with taxes) is certain. But would it not be more appropriate to say that the one thing most *un*certain for a believer (as we approach the end of the age) is death? Millions of Christians now living may *never* die!

The dead in Christ shall rise first (they have six feet further to travel, as James McGinlay used to remind us), and then we in Christ who are alive and remain shall be caught up TOGETHER to meet the Lord in the air.

We need not sorrow as those who have no hope—for we *do* have a hope! But Christians do sometimes have sorrow. "Many are the afflictions of the righteous," David reminded us in Psalm 34:18. But for the believer, as Spurgeon put it, "Sorrow and trouble are sometimes the black horse upon which mercy rides to the door." Christians are always looking forward to a better day and to a glad reunion.

> In the resurrection morning, what a meeting it will be,
>   We shall rise, Hallelujah, we shall rise!
> When our fathers and our mothers, and our loved ones
>   we shall see,
>   We shall rise. . .We shall rise!

An uncle of mine, once a chaplain for the prison system in a state up East, told of an old man who had been saved but who, though dying, was always praising the Lord. Gangrene had poisoned his body, and the doctors said he was a "goner." He told the chaplain, "You can pray for me, but on one condition: don't pray for me to *live.* I've looked forward to seeing my Lord for a long time now." The next day he was gone, but gone to be with the Lord forever. How much *more* wonderful to have Him come for *us* and meet Him in the air *without* dying?

I'll see my mother again in that glad day of reunion and rapture. My dad, whose funeral I (along with my two preacher brothers) conducted, will be no longer dead in that glorious morning. That beloved missionary I had led to the Lord and later had to bury, will be alive forevermore! The man who accepted Christ as I stood by his hospital bed in Panama City, after he had been horribly burned in an accident, will be very much alive and without his scars, in a perfect body. H. V. Lemley, my beloved missionary brother, who has labored in Mexico now for many years without the cheering help and encouragement of his departed wife, will suddenly have her at his side again, and forever! Oh, glorious daybreak!

III. A THIRD JOY OF THE SECOND COMING WILL BE THE RICH REWARDS AWAITING THOSE WHO HAVE FAITHFULLY SERVED HIM.

When Paul came to the end of the way and was facing execution for no greater crime than that of preaching Christ, he cried, "Henceforth there is laid up for me a crown of righteousness, which the Lord, the righteous judge, shall give me *at that day.*" He knew he would not be rewarded immediately when he went into the presence of Christ, for he would have to await the Judgment Seat of Christ, yet future, which takes place after the rapture of the church. Paul could not have been rewarded *then* for he is still accumulating rewards from the saints today who are being inspired by his life and his writings!

So even as the wicked are treasuring up wrath against the day of wrath, so the Christian is accumulating rewards as he faithfully serves the Saviour here. "We must all appear before the judgment seat of Christ," Paul declares in II Corinthians 5:10. I think it was Dr. McGee who reminded us that the word "appear" in this verse means not only to show up but to be shown up. It does matter how a Christian lives! The more obedient and dedicated we are as Christians, the more joy we have over the prospect of the Lord's return and the judgment seat.

"Behold, I come quickly; and my reward is with me, to give every man according as his work shall be" (Rev. 22:12). Paul encouraged Corinthian Christians to live for the Lord so that they would "come behind in no gift; waiting for the coming of our Lord Jesus Christ: Who shall also confirm you unto the end, that ye may be blameless in the day of our Lord Jesus Christ" (I Cor. 1:7,8).

Rewards will be our portion for loving His appearing (II Tim. 4:8); for enduring temptation (James 1:12); for running the race of life with temperance and discipline (I Cor. 9:24,25); for being good examples (I Pet. 5:3,4); and for winning souls (I Thess. 2:19,20). Here in this last verse the very word JOY is used in relation to the second coming. Perhaps God would have us know that those who will *most* enjoy the return of Christ will be those who have others ready to go into Heaven with Him at the rapture, too!

IV. A FOURTH JOY PROMISED IN RELATION TO HIS RETURN IS TRUE SATISFACTION.

Who is really satisfied except the one who knows Christ? I stepped into an elevator in a Chattanooga hotel. A simple but sweet and saintly black woman was working the elevator. Being the only passenger on board that trip I said a word for the Lord and asked her if she knew the Lord as her Saviour. She replied, "Sho *nuff* I do," and with a look of bliss on her face, she beamed, "I'm ready to say it this mawning! *Sho* nuff I *do!*" She left me in no doubt that she really had found satisfaction in the Lord.

A sports fan on the way home from the defeat of his University of Georgia football team in the Sugar Bowl of 1983 was among those stung by defeat who, they said, "could only grope in the dark." "We've been drunk for three days," the football enthusiast moaned, "I don't know what it would be like to be sober again." So if a man's life is *sports* and his team is defeated, he has no satisfaction.

The sinner talks about getting stoned, feeling no pain, out of it, smashed, tanked, soused, high, pickled and stewed. But through it all he has no satisfaction. These are different ways of describing the common drunk. The world is full of them.

They can talk about getting high or getting gassed. They can call it getting wiped out or tying one on; but it is still just plain old messy, nasty, stinking, stupid drunkenness. They have no satisfaction in life, and they just want to get "out of it."

When the Queen of Sheba came to Solomon, she found more than she had ever imagined a king could have. "The half had never been told" me, she admitted (see I Kings 10). But what of those who have found true satisfaction in great Solomon's greater Son, the Lord Jesus?

> To Jesus every day I find my heart is closer drawn;
>   He's fairer than the glory of the gold and purple dawn;
> He's all my fancy pictures in its fairest dreams and more;
>   Each day He grows still sweeter than He was the day before.
> The half cannot be fancied this side the golden shore,
>   Oh, there He'll be still sweeter than He ever was before.
>   —W. C. Martin

Yes, Christ is not a disappointment. And we'll find even a greater measure of satisfaction when we see Him face to face. "As for me, I will behold thy face in righteousness: I shall be *satisfied*, when I awake, with thy likeness" (Ps. 17:15).

We are satisfied with His salvation. "My soul shall be satisfied" (Ps. 63:5).

We are satisfied with His mercy (Ps. 90:14).

Generally the clean Christian will outlive the sinner, and He thus satisfies us with "long life" (see Ps. 91:16).

He satisfies us with good things along the way (Ps. 103:5). How *good* the Lord is!

He that has the fear of the Lord "will abide satisfied" (Prov. 19:23).

But best of all, we'll be satisfied when we see Him at His coming (Ps. 17:15). "I will see you again, and your heart shall rejoice, and your joy no man taketh from you" (John 16:22). Oh, the joy of the second coming!

V. RECOGNITION IN HEAVEN IS ANOTHER JOY OF HIS RETURN.

Since Heaven is a very real place where we shall see clearly (not through a glass darkly—I Cor. 13:12) and we shall know as we are known, then quite obviously we are going to enjoy recognition of our own loved ones as well as others we would like to know in Heaven. God would not have us to be ignorant, Paul advises in I Thessalonians 4:13, about those who are asleep in Jesus. We need not sorrow as those do who have no hope. Unsaved people tell their loved ones good-bye for the last time. There is nothing sadder than the funeral of a sinner, wept over by relatives who are lost and have no hope.

This recognition and reunion of loved ones relates to His return; for in verse 14 of I Thessalonians 4, Paul writes, "For if we believe that Jesus died and rose again, even so them also which sleep in Jesus will God bring with him." Now what good on earth could it possibly do to tell Christians that their loved ones would be brought back with Him (and that we could not precede the bodies of those still sleeping in the graves) if we were not going to *know* those loved ones when (in our glorified bodies) we are "caught up together with them in the clouds to meet the Lord in the air"?

In verse 17 He tells us we'll be "caught up together" with those who have gone on before, and then verse 18 says, "Wherefore *comfort* one another with these words." This has given much comfort to many a mother who has lost her child, or to many a wife who has lost her husband, and to many a man whose wife has been taken from him by cancer. But there would be no comfort if we would not even recognize our own loved ones when Jesus comes again.

Two children stood outside a bakery looking at the good things in the display window. They were very poor and could never have delightful pastries like their mouths watered for. It was always so. When they looked at toys, it was always through the windows.

When they saw pretty new clothes, it was always through the glass.

A wealthy and generous man saw the children at the bakery window, and his heart was touched. He took the grimy little hands in his and led them into the store. There they saw the cookies and cakes and cream puffs on the counter before them as the kind man told them to help themselves. They could hardly believe their eyes. They could scarcely believe that they could actually put out their hands and *touch* the sweet delicacies. "Look, Johnny," the little girl gleefully exclaimed, "there's no glass between!"

Well, thank God, though "now we see through a glass darkly," one of these days we'll see Him and our loved ones who have died in the Lord and there will be NO GLASS BETWEEN!

VI. STILL ANOTHER JOY WILL BE THAT OF FINAL VICTORY OVER THE DEVIL.

Down here it is a battle. The fiery darts of Satan are constantly flung at us. We live in a world that has been dominated by him who is accepted by people all about us as "the god of this world" (II Cor. 4:4). He is the prince of the power of the air (Eph. 2:2). We, in this life, feel the "fury of the oppressor" (Isa. 51:13). We smart under his foul dominion. We cringe at the language, laughter, music and conversation of his cohorts—the wicked all around us. We know that we don't belong down here. This world is not our home. Here we have no continuing city. Our citizenship is in Heaven. We lament the fact that Satan's heroes, whether they be in the athletic, the political or the entertainment world, are the ones lauded and applauded down here, while the *real* heroes, God's choice servants, are ignored, despised and ridiculed, if not actually done away with.

But one day it will all be different. This fiendish rebel, Satan, will be taken as a dragon or a terrible serpent (for that he is) and will be bound for a thousand years (Rev. 20:2). He will be held in a bottomless pit. At the end of the thousand years, he will be released for a little season as man's final test. But the deceiver, the Devil, will once again be taken by divine power and cast into the lake of fire and brimstone (Rev. 20:10) "and shall be tormented day and night for ever and ever." What a commentary on Satan and his follies and followers. There cannot be anything for him (nor for those who follow him) but eternal burnings!

So, child of God, remember, "the God of peace shall bruise Satan under your feet shortly" (see Rom. 16:20). Life's constant struggle and battle will be done at Christ's second coming.

Meantime, though we cannot be absent from Satan's world, we can even now enjoy a great measure of victory over Him through Christ who dwells within us. Someone knocked on Martin Luther's door after his conversion and asked, "Does Martin Luther live here?" His reply was, "No, CHRIST LIVES HERE!"

In the book that records the demise of Satan and his removal from our domain, we can even now read, "And they overcame him [the Devil] by the blood of the Lamb, and by the word of their testimony; and they loved not their lives unto the death" (Rev. 12:11). You can fight the good fight of faith and endure the onslaughts of Satan a bit longer as you realize that his promised capture and destruction will be a reality when Jesus comes. He that is with us is mightier than he that is against us.

An Ohio pastor where I conducted a meeting in 1981 took me out to see the world's largest mobile land machine, a towering triumph of American technology, which they call Big Muskie. This monster machine was the biggest movable thing I've ever seen. It is used to scoop out mountains of dirt and rock and dig down to the coal in southeastern Ohio near the West Virginia line. The housing alone on this hulking earthmover is about the size of a six-story apartment building. Muskie takes huge gargantuan steps, munches 325 tons of dirt in one bite and generates the power of 63,000 horses. It is the world's biggest and most powerful strip miner. It weighs 27 million pounds, more than most U. S. Navy cruisers, more than 128 Boeing 727 jets. The bucket on this monster can scoop up in one bite the weight of 10 railroad box cars. That single scoop can fill more than 20 dump trucks. A big Ohio high school band has stood inside Muskie's huge bucket! It was an awe-inspiring thing to look at.

But then I thought of the power of God and realized that one day Big Muskie will melt and crumble when God stretches forth His mighty hand to reduce this present world system to rubble, and "there will be new heavens and a new earth wherein dwelleth righteousness!" Oh, glorious day! And a God like that can even now give us day-by-day victory over sin and Satan.

VII. FINALLY, THE JOY OF THE SECOND COMING IS THE TRIUMPH OF HEAVEN AND OUR PROMISED PLACE OF ETERNAL REST.

All of this and more will be our portion when He who said, "In my Father's house are many mansions. . .I go to prepare a place for you and. . .will come again to receive you unto myself" does make good on His promise and shows up for us in that glad day.

He will return to avenge His cross. He will set things right once again. Paradise will be restored as He deals in judgment with the wicked and banishes all unbelievers and unrighteous ones from His earth. God will then once again take possession. The triumph of Heaven and the terrors of Hell will be finally and irrevocably established.

On his morning talk show, Phil Donahue recently was giving some Christians a hard time, especially when they admitted to believing in a burning Hell. Donahue declared, "If I were God, I would have to be a bit more *merciful* than that!" (Sinners can never understand how there could be a Hell for they cannot understand the awful enormity of sin and the magnificent holiness of God.) Then Donahue said, "Now really, don't you think when we get up there He'll say to all of us, 'Oh, *all right*—just *come* on *in*'?" That's the way the unregenerate mind tries to figure it out.

But suppose God did give in (an impossibility) and say to all sinners, "Oh, all right, just come on in to my Heaven." What they do not understand is that if God allowed that, Heaven would soon be as full of sin and lust and evil and misery and torture and death as this old sin-cursed earth is now. Heaven would soon be Hell!

No, "the fearful, and unbelieving, and the abominable, and murderers, and whoremongers, and sorcerers, and idolaters, and all liars, shall have their part in the lake which burneth with fire and brimstone: which is the second death" (Rev. 21:8).

God will have no beer cans on the celestial shores; no pornography in the Heavenly bookshelves; no booze on the dining table of the ivory palaces; and no profanity turning blue the rarefied air of the New Jerusalem.

There will be no more poverty, no more pain, no more perplexities. God will wipe away all tears. He will never again tolerate wars and crime and human anguish. There shall be no more curse. No darkness there. No filth, no vulgarity, no carnality. "There shall in no wise enter into it anything that defileth, neither whatsoever worketh abomination, or maketh a lie: but they which are written in the Lamb's book of life" (Rev. 21:27).

I read that a man once came running to Emerson crying, "O Mr. Emerson, the world is coming to an end!" The reply was, "Oh, well. Let it come. I can get along without it."

Christians can get along without this world as we revel in His rich promises of the world to come. But in the meantime, may our hearts be broken for the great mass of mankind who do not know our Saviour. "Where Jesus is 'tis Heaven," so we must get them to Jesus so they'll be ready for His return.

William Burns became a great preacher because he said as a child he kept hearing the thud of Christless feet on the way to a Christless Hell.

A friend of ours who is an interior decorator told us of the sorrow that came to a family whose home she had decorated in a stylish part of a beautiful southern neighborhood. Their seventeen-year-old daughter was a brilliant girl, already a premed student in a famous university. Her parents were very successful. They had lavished gifts upon their daughter, including a new car. They lived in an exquisite home. The girl had seemed to be happy.

But one day soon after an elaborate Christmas they found her lying down in the closed garage under the car with the engine running. Her suicide had been planned carefully. She had left an explanatory note. She just couldn't do everything she wanted to do and felt that she could not cope with life. So a beautiful child joined the thousands of others who take their own lives every year in our society. A young friend of hers later remarked that she (the suicide) "has just done what I didn't have the guts to do!"

There you have it. We can rejoice in the golden promises of His sure return. Ours is the joy of the second coming. But multitudes around us do not have this joy, this peace, this assurance. Prophetic knowledge should be matched with practical duty. He who is coming is the one and only preparation for His coming. Clad in His righteousness alone are we faultless to stand before His throne. Let us tell this glorious good news quickly. The King's business requireth haste!

CHAPTER 10

The Transforming Hope of His Return

"To serve the living and true God; And to wait for his Son from heaven."—I Thess. 1:9,10.

On the sugary white sands of the gulf shore I've seen some beautiful sand castles. They have been constructed with great patience and much care. But a few hours later the tide comes in and the castles crumble, dissolve and disappear. So I've never spent much time working on sand castles.

Most people, even some Christians, are spending most of their time working on things that will soon crumble and fade away. How sad. Life is so short and human need so great that it behooves Christians to find out what things are truly important and will be most richly rewarded.

"Blessed is that servant, whom his lord when he cometh shall find so doing" (Luke 12:43). How vital the stewardship of our time!

The personal return of Christ for His own is perhaps the most commanding incentive of all to holy living and dedicated service. Paul in the verse quoted at the beginning of this chapter told the Thessalonian Christians to turn to God from idols and serve the living God while waiting for His Son from Heaven. God knows we need motivation—something to keep us stirred up to give Him our best while here in this pagan world. So He sends us one beautiful promise and challenge after another about the second coming of Christ to accomplish this. "This same Jesus shall come," "I will come again," "The Lord himself shall descend from heaven with a shout," "Be ye therefore ready," and on and on. Then He links these wonderful promises with Christian service and duty to make our work easier, our load lighter and our future brighter.

> **Be not a-weary, for labor will cease,**
> **Some glad morning;**
> **Turmoil will change into infinite peace,**
> **Some bright morning.**
> —C. G. Homer

We are to be doers of the Word and not hearers only. The mystery from above works best in the misery below. Christians are happiest when they are busy—"fervent in spirit; serving the Lord" (Rom. 12:11). And nothing so spurs us on as the vivid assurance that soon we will stand before Him and give an account of our labor, service and stewardship. Observe first of all that the blessed hope draws us to church for

I. FAITHFULNESS IN WORSHIP.

Hebrews 10:24 urges us to consider one another to provoke unto love and to good works, and in order to do this God says, "Not forsaking the assembling of ourselves together, as the manner of some is; but exhorting one another: and so much the more, as ye see the day approaching" (Heb. 10:25). Thus we see that the approaching day of the coming of Christ is a great incentive to be in our places in good churches, not only because we need spiritual food and fellowship, but because we are to "consider one another" and exhort (or encourage) one another in view of the Lord's return. Other Christians need to see us there. It helps them and it pleases the Lord. And this is true all the more, God says, as you see the day approaching. In this dark, dangerous and distressful time, we need one another; and we need the Lord, and He needs us!

Absenteeism is a problem in business and industry. It is even a greater problem in the work of the Lord. Thomas missed the first Sunday night service after the resurrection. No wonder he became "doubting" Thomas!

Weak Christians come to church. They realize other saints who are supposedly strong Christians are absent, and it is a stumblingblock to them. You are the best Christian somebody knows. They are watching us. We provoke others to love and to good works by our own faithfulness. We are to encourage one another by being together in loving fellowship and service in view of His soon coming.

Again, the second coming of Christ is an incentive to

II. LOVE ONE ANOTHER.

I Thessalonians 3:12,13 states, "And the Lord make you to increase and abound in love one toward another, and toward all men, even as we do toward you: To the end he may stablish your hearts unblameable in holiness before God, even our Father, *at the coming* of our Lord Jesus Christ. . . ."

It is so sad that some Christians bite and devour one another. Just because the liberals and false religionists talk "love" and ooze "brotherhood" all the time does not excuse the bickering and backbiting and jealousy seen in the lives of so many fundamental Christians. Jesus did say, "A new commandment I give unto you, That ye love one another. . ." (John 13:34). God does command us to "love one another with a pure heart fervently" (I Pet. 1:22b). And the reminder that soon we must all face Him at the judgment seat and give an account of ourselves (not of the other fellow) should sober us indeed!

This is not to say that we are to embrace error or compromise with evil. Jesus told us to beware of wolves in sheep's clothing. But this does not prevent our fellowship with others of like precious faith with whom we may sometimes disagree, or with those who may use methods that we could not in good conscience use ourselves. Paul wrote, "Who art thou that judgest another man's servant? to his own master he standeth or falleth" (Rom. 14:4). Soon the Lord will come and straighten out all the differences. Meanwhile, we are to increase and abound in love one toward another, and toward all men, according to the verses above quoted in I Thessalonians 3:12,13.

In our fundamental churches, Christians can often be very cruel to one another. Unkind slurs, cutting jibes and critical remarks are frequently heard by Christians talking about other believers in the church. I've heard Christians say that they have received kinder treatment where they work in the unsaved world than they do when they come to their own church on Sunday! And that is a sad state of affairs. The church should be a haven, a place of refreshment and restoration. If we live like we should and seek souls for the Master, we receive enough sneers, ridicule, and misunderstanding from the world all week. We should be able to know that when we come to the house of God, the saints will be glad to see us and will receive us warmly with Christian courtesy and love. We all need the prayers, the concern, the sympathy and the encouragement of other believers. And as nears our Lord's return we are going to need one another all the more. Since the Devil knows that he has but a short time (see Revelation 12:12), he is increasing the pressure on the saints all the time.

Christians "fall out" with one another over the slightest disagreements oftentimes. Before the nuclear "fall out" from the coming holocaust hits this world, we Christians need to "fall in" and march together in the army of the Lord! Satan is our common enemy. Let us not spend our sojourn here firing on our own soldiers!

III. THE COMING OF CHRIST SHOULD BE OUR INCENTIVE TO PATIENCE.

"Be patient therefore, brethren, unto the coming of the Lord. Behold, the husbandman waiteth for the precious fruit of the earth, and hath long patience for it, until he receive the early and latter rain. Be ye also patient; stablish your hearts: for the coming of the Lord draweth nigh."—James 5:7,8.

Many of us are like the man who prayed, "Give me patience, Lord, but hurry!" How jumpy and jittery we are. How seldom do we find believers really resting in the Lord and waiting patiently for Him. We stay "in a fizz," as my Dad used to put it. Note that James said in connection with patience, "stablish your hearts." As we become mature and established in our walk with God and in our understanding of His Word, we should determine to stand upon His promises with patience and let God work in His own good way.

And no matter how rough it gets down here, we can be patient because we know that our Saviour is soon coming. "For ye have need of patience, that, after ye have done the will of God, ye might receive the promise. For yet a little while, and he that shall come will come, and will not tarry" (Heb. 10:36,37).

Peter reminds us in his first epistle that we sometimes are in heaviness through manifold temptations. But then he goes on, "That the trial of your faith, being much more precious than of gold that perisheth, though it be tried with fire, might be found unto praise and honour and glory *at the appearing of Jesus Christ*" (I Pet. 1:7). So we can be patient in our trials since the coming of the Lord will make it all clear, and "we'll understand it better by and by."

IV. HIS COMING SHOULD INSPIRE US TO ABIDE IN CHRIST.

See I John 2:28, "And now, little children, abide in him; that, when he shall appear, we may have confidence, and not be ashamed before him at his coming." If we are abiding in Him, then we will not be embarrassed by having Him return and find us doing something He would be ashamed to find us doing. And we would not be disgraced by being found in a place where He would not go.

"Abide in me, and I in you. As the branch cannot bear fruit of itself, except it abide in the vine; no more can ye, except ye abide in me," said Jesus in John 15:4. In verse eight of that same chapter, He tells us that the Father is glorified as we bear much fruit. But this whole first part of John 15 is written to tell us that we will not thus be bearing fruit unless we abide in Christ. Only then will we have confidence at His second coming and not be ashamed when we see Him face to face.

We must all appear before the judgment seat of Christ where we will be rewarded or suffer loss of reward (see I Cor. 3; Rom. 14:10; II Cor. 5:10). People in an office are on their best behavior when they know the boss is about to appear on the scene. How much more should we live on our best behavior as we realize that Christ may appear at any moment.

When Dwight Eisenhower was President, he once, during an election year, made a sudden and unannounced tour through a Washington residential district meeting people as he knocked on the doors of private dwellings. People would look up in amazement to find the President of the United States standing on the doormat. One woman, when she saw who it was, cried out, "Oh, Mr. President, if I had known *you* were coming I would have cleaned up today!" Well, we KNOW the Lord is coming so we had better clean up our lives and "abide in Him." If we hold forth the Word of life, we will one day be able to rejoice in the day of Christ that we have not run in vain nor labored in vain, Paul assures us in Philippians 2:16.

V. THE COMING OF OUR LORD IS ALSO A COMMANDING INCENTIVE TO PREACH THE WORD.

Preachers and teachers should listen to Peter when he cries, "*Feed* the flock of God which is among you, taking the oversight thereof. . . . And when the chief Shepherd shall appear, ye shall receive a crown of glory that fadeth not away" (I Pet. 5:2,4).

Paul spoke of Christ coming to judge the quick and the dead in II Timothy 4, reminding preachers to be faithful to "preach the word; be instant in season, out of season; reprove, rebuke, exhort with all longsuffering and doctrine. For the time will come when they will not endure sound doctrine." So the imminent return of Christ should make us alert to be faithful to declare the whole counsel of God. One day we will report to Him and give account of ourselves at His coming.

Jude (v. 3) adds to that by commanding us to "earnestly contend for the faith which was once delivered unto the saints," and warns us of ungodly men who will "creep in" to the church and turn the grace of God into lasciviousness and deny the Lord. He calls them "raging waves of the sea, foaming out their own shame; wandering stars, to whom is reserved the blackness of darkness for ever" (Jude 13).

Those who criticize Jesus, play down the Word, compromise with sin, and feed the people on the husks of this world instead of the Book will be in for a terrifying surprise when Jesus comes!

One high school girl said after a preacher had brought a good message at a chapel service, "Most of the *preachers* who come here just tell us a lot of funny stories." What a menu for spiritually starved souls!

VI. HIS COMING IS ALSO AN INCENTIVE TO WATCHFULNESS IN PRAYER.

"But the end of all things is at hand: be ye therefore sober, and watch unto prayer."—I Pet. 4:7.

Because He is coming soon we should be much in prayer.

And we should be very watchful, for "your adversary the devil, as a roaring lion, walketh about, seeking whom he may devour" (I Pet. 5:8).

"Watch ye therefore: for ye know not when the master of the house cometh."—Mark 13:35.

"Therefore let us not sleep, as do others; but let us watch and be sober."—I Thess. 5:6.

". . .it is high time to awake out of sleep: for now is our salvation nearer than when we believed. The night is far spent, the day is at hand: let us therefore cast off the works of darkness, and let us put on the armour of light."—Rom. 13:11-12.

Watch out for the wiles of the Devil. In these days, *opportunity* merely knocks: the *Devil* kicks the door in! "Watch and pray!"

VII. HIS COMING, TOO, IS AN INCENTIVE TO SEPARATION.

We are to *"turn from idols* to serve the living God and to wait for His Son from Heaven," according to Paul's letter to the Thessalonians.

Jesus said, "And take heed to yourselves, lest at any time your hearts be overcharged with surfeiting, and drunkenness, and cares of this life, and so that day come upon you unawares" (Luke 21:34).

So in view of His return we are to live separated Christian lives. We are not to go around with headaches from over-indulgences. We are to be in command of our ships, disciplining ourselves to resist the allurements of a God-hating world and a lust-laden society. The people who came over with Columbus had to leave the old world behind to enjoy the challenge and bounty and beauty of the new world. *We* are to be separated from the old and put on the new man—in view of His coming.

When I stay in a motel for a week while holding a revival, I do not fix up the room, hang pictures, plant flowers around the door, or move new furniture into the cubicle. Why? There is nothing wrong with these things; but I am only there as a so-journer, as a temporary resident. Soon I'll be off to another place. Even so, our citizenship is in Heaven. We don't belong down here.

We are to "approve things that are excellent; that ye may be sincere and without offence till the day of Christ" (Phil. 1:10). We are to deny ungodliness and worldly lusts while we look for His Son from Heaven, Paul wrote to Titus.

Separation is not a popular teaching in this modern age of compromise, but God still says, "Ye adulterers and adulteresses, know ye not that the friendship of the world is enmity with God? whosoever therefore will be a friend of the world is the enemy of God" (James 4:4).

We need to be very careful about letting the world seep into our lives, our homes and our churches. A Texas pastor told me that he saw that television was taking up too much time in his home and that the influence of it was affecting his children. So they removed the set from the home and very carefully weaned the family from it. After several months when the family was strong and realized that they could live without it, they made a contract to allow it back in the home *only* on the condition that the set was very carefully monitored and used only for rare and special programs, sporting events or newscasts that were approved by the parents. There once was a time when worldliness meant going out into the world. Now with television, the world will come in to us unless we are decidedly disciplined.

VIII. AGAIN, HIS RETURN IS AN INCENTIVE TO PURITY OF LIFE.

"Every man that hath this hope in him purifieth *himself, even as he is pure."*—I John 3:3.

We put on our best for a coming guest, especially a very important guest of renown. "Wherefore gird up the loins of your mind, be sober, and hope to the end for the grace that is to be brought unto you at the revelation of Jesus Christ; As obedient children, not fashioning yourselves according to the former lusts in your ignorance: But as he which hath called you is holy, so be ye holy in all manner of conversation" (I Pet. 1:13-15).

When I was a small boy, we lived for a time in a Maryland town. My dad got a better job in Pennsylvania probably about 100 miles or more away. For many weeks until school was out, he would come home on Friday night or Saturday morning and stay with the family until Sunday evening before catching the train back to his job. I loved my dad, and I looked forward to his coming each weekend. One Friday my mother got me bathed and into fresh, clean clothes so I would be ready for Dad's return. But I got to playing down in the basement and decided to surprise Dad by painting the basement wall for him. When he arrived, the basement was ruined; the paint was ruined, and my clothes were ruined. My dad was a cleaner. He took me to the cleaners in more ways than one! I was ashamed before him at his coming. His return which should have been such a happy occasion for me turned out to be a reunion of shame and chastening.

We should "be diligent that ye may be found of him in peace, without spot, and blameless" (II Pet. 3:14).

By the books we read, the programs we watch, the music we listen to, the crowd we run with, sometimes even the church we attend, our worldliness is measured.

IX. THE SECOND COMING, TOO, IS A MIGHTY INCENTIVE TO SOUL WINNING.

While waiting we are to serve Him, and how better to do this than by being engaged in the business God is most interested in—the soul-winning business? "Why stand ye gazing up into heaven," the disciples were asked in Acts 1:11. Christ had ascended, the Holy Spirit was about to descend. In the same verse they were assured (and we are) that Christ ("This same Jesus") will come again. Since His return will mean judgment for the unsaved, we need to get them into the ark of safety before that day of His appearing.

Jude, in the prophetic book just before Revelation, urges us to have compassion and save souls "with fear, pulling them out of the fire" (Jude 22,23). In *Reader's Digest* the heroic story is told of a Maryland man who saved the lives of four teenagers from a burning wreck, literally "pulling them out of the fire." He received national recognition and praise. How much more should we be diligent to snatch souls from the flames by bringing them to Christ before the wrath of God falls upon them.

We are to study the Word of God not to win arguments but to win souls. We are not to get so enthralled with trying to figure out all of the toes on the foot of some prophetic beast that we never move either foot to go bring some perishing sinner to the Saviour.

When He comes back, the crown of rejoicing will be given to the person who has invested his life in this glorious task of winning souls (see I Thess. 2:19,20). What a transforming hope—this promise of His return!

As this is being written, the country is observing "Ground Zero week," thus trying to alert the American people to the possibilities and to the terrors of nuclear war. We are being told that young children are afraid, that teens are plunging into sin feeling that it will soon be all over anyway, and that many adults are living in terror about the impending doom. What a time to point these poor, fearful souls to the Son of God. Never should it be easier to let them know that the worst will come after the rapture, that Jesus is coming soon, and that there is a way *out* by coming to Christ in true repentance and faith, and thus be ready for His return. This thing is marked urgent. It may soon be all over. "Be ye therefore ready!"

CHAPTER 11

The Answer Is in the Back of the Book

The old math books presented the problems to be solved on the lesson pages. They also contained the answers to these problems—in the back of the book. And woe be unto the student who was caught looking in the back of the book before he was told to!

I have always enjoyed a good mystery story. And though I seldom read fiction anymore, I do recall the suspense of some of those stories, and how difficult it sometimes was to wait until I got to the end of the book to see how it all came out. Some people, I am told, look in the last chapter to find out what is going to happen, then go back and read the book. That would take all the fun out of it for me. But at least that reader did not have to bite his or her fingernails and stay in a state of suspension while the hero or heroine hung by a thread from a cliff. For he had read ahead and knew that it was all going to be all right when the story was finished. The hero would be vindicated, the criminal properly sentenced; the family would move to the beautiful home on the top of the hill, and the heroine would have her dreamed-of wedding. They would all live happily ever after!

It is so today in real life. Never have Christians been so full of frustration and suspense about our plight in this life. Never has the villain (Satan) seemed to have such power. Never has there been so much threat of impending doom. But the child of God can have the answers about how it is all going to come out. He can look in the back of the Book!

The book of Revelation contains the explanation of why many things have gone before. All that begins with man in Genesis, ends in Revelation. The trauma and tragedy of human life finds its consummation in the last book of the Bible. Indeed, the answer is in the back of the Book! So while people of the world, even the learned ones, are struggling with the great problems and burdens of life and society, the child of God can go confidently and cheerfully forward; for he knows that a brighter day is just ahead. The answer is in the back of the Book!

Computer scientists ten years ago warned that the world is running out of everything, including time. They have just made a new assessment. Their bleak predictions are the same—except now its ten years closer. The Club of Rome gathered for these conclusions at the Smithsonian Museum of Natural History.

A Ban-the-Bomb Movement is underway at present as thousands of Americans are storming through the streets urging us to get rid of our bombs or cease making them. A recent twist is to promise Russia and the world that we will never make the first nuclear strike. This, of course, would mean that we'd have to fight Russia (or other enemy nations) with conventional weapons and that no matter how many of our allies fell under the bloody mauling of communism, we'd still have to be calm and let the takeover go on since we had promised not to strike first with the kind of weapon that could show that we mean business.

Even some preachers and religious leaders who ought surely to know better are urging us to stop building up our defenses and trust Russia to do the same! Many liberal students today are insisting that we get rid of our nuclear weapons altogether! This, of course, is tantamount to saying, "Let's all make up our minds that when Russia wants us, she can have us. We'd rather be red than dead."

Maybe that doesn't sound like too bad an idea for people who are godless and atheistic anyway and who are amoral, if not immoral. But people of character who believe in God, morality, and freedom do not want to spend the rest of their lives as slaves to Moscow! And saved people who know what the Bible teaches are aware of the fact that the *worst* of what lies ahead is going to happen *after* Christ comes for His own and we are taken *out* of this world. So the controversy rages on.

All of this poses many questions, and some of them are being asked even by Christians. The answers to the most perplexing of these are to be found in the back of the Book—in the book of Revelation.

Revelation is the book of the returning King.

It is the only book that promises a special blessing to those who read and hear and keep the things written in the book (see Rev. 1:3).

It leads to the reign of Christ over the earth that Satan has determined all these years to rule (Rev. 11:15).

It describes the Devil's defeat and doom.

Revelation is not a riddle but an unveiling. Most of it is yet to be fulfilled.

It is the Revelation of Jesus Christ, not of the church, or John (the human author), or some other man (see Rev. 1:1).

It deals with His glorious return to set things right. "The time is at hand" (Rev. 1:3b).

Revelation is the climax of the great drama of all ages. The hero is the Lord Himself. The villain is the Devil. The Antichrist stalks across the stage. Through blood and fire, brimstone and plague, earthquake and flood, trials and terrors, the book announces the doom of man and his efforts to rule himself apart from God.

The outline of this last book of the Bible is to be found in Revelation 1:19 where we learn that God deals with the things already seen (past), the things that are now (the church age), and then the things which shall be hereafter (future things). From chapter 4 to the end it deals with the future.

Many of the most-often-asked questions find their answers in the back of the Book—in the book of Revelation! For instance

(1) *How can His coming be secret if every eye shall see Him?*

Well, the Bible does say that every eye shall see Him (Rev. 1:7). But this is the second and main phase of His return. This points to His glorious advent when He comes all the way down to the earth and establishes His kingdom. At that point, of course, everyone will see Him; and all will know He is here. But at least seven years earlier, He will have come in the clouds to catch His waiting bride, the church, away "until the indignation (of the Great Tribulation) be overpast." (For this rapture or first phase of His return, see Isa. 26:19,20; Acts 1:11; John 14:3; I Thess. 4:16,17; Titus 2:13; I Cor. 15:51-53; Phil. 3:20,21).

The advent of Revelation 1:7 is the *revelation* of Christ or His return in glory when He comes back *with* His saints—the blood-washed armies of Heaven. (See II Thess. 1:8; Jude 14,15; II Pet. 3:12; Isa. 66:15,16; Matt. 24:27; Zech. 14:3-9; Rev. 19:11-16.) Distinguish between the two phases of His second coming and the whole picture becomes clear. Do away with the rapture and try to make all of the second coming verses blend into one event and you have a jumble of impossibilities!

(2) *How do we know who Jesus really is?*

The world has argued back and forth. He has been called Son of God, Son of man, great teacher, religious leader, miracle-worker, pacifist, imposter, fraud—you name it! But, really, who *is* He? The whole Bible reveals Him and is written about Him, but the final answer is in the back of the Book.

In Revelation 1:18 He declares Himself to be the resurrected Saviour who was dead and now is alive forevermore with the keys of Hell and death. In Revelation 4:11 He is seen to be the Lord of glory, receiving glory and honor and power, the One who created all things for His own pleasure. Thus He is the Creator-God of John 1 who 'made all things and without whom there was nothing made that was made!' He is the One of whom Paul wrote in Colossians 1:16, "For by him were all things created, that are in heaven, and that are in earth, visible and invisible, whether they be thrones, or dominions, or principalities, or powers: all things were created by him, and for him."

To go back to the back of the Book, in Revelation 5 we find Him to be the Lion of the tribe of Juda, the Root of David (vs. 5), the Lamb who has been slain (vs. 6), the One who redeemed us to God by His blood out of every kindred and tongue and people and nation (vs. 9). In chapter 6 we find that He is the Saviour-God sitting on the throne while the great men and kings of this earth will cry for rocks and mountains to fall on them and hide them from the face of Christ in the day of His great wrath (vs. 17). Jesus is God the Son, no less God than God the Father is God!

(3) *What has happened to the Church?*

The answer is in the back of the Book. In the 19th century and in the first forty years of this century, the church did wield a great influence and power. The entire church age is found in miniature in the seven churches of Revelation 2 and 3. The influence of Rome and the pagan world is seen in Pergamos, Thyatira and Sardis. Many of those years in the history of the church did indeed constitute the dark ages. Then came Philadelphia when godly men discovered the open door of verse 8 in Revelation 3 and found that no man could shut it.

In those days Christians kept His Word and did not deny His name (vs. 8). These were the days of Spurgeon, Moody, Finney, Wesley, Whitefield, William Munsey and A. B. Earle. Those were the days that marked the great missionary thrust of David Livingstone, Hudson Taylor, Judson, and Carey. The church was still packing a mighty wallop in the early days of the 20th century with the revivals of Sam Jones, Billy Sunday and J. Wilbur Chapman. And there were still strong rivers of blessing flowing in the ministries of such men as R. A. Torrey, Bob Jones, Sr., Harry Ironside, Mordecai Ham, Charles E. Fuller, M. R. DeHaan, and John R. Rice. By now the floodtide of modernism had begun in earnest. Many colleges and theological institutions, once sound and fundamental, began to waver. Soon came Neo-orthodoxy, then the new evangelicalism, then the clear lines of demarcation and separation began to fade.

Still there was much blessing as God raised up schools like Bob Jones University and Tennessee Temple University. *The Sword of the Lord,* edited by Dr. John Rice, became a mighty influence for God, for evangelism and for separated Christian living. God put His mighty hand on numerous pastors and evangelists. Various independent Baptist and Bible movements are still being blessed of God.

Meanwhile, many groups and denominations have become so institutionalized and so compromised that they hardly resemble what they once were. In many cases, religious publishing houses that once could be trusted to produce sound, fundamental literature, are now printing shallow and powerless material, while others are giving in to the charismatic clamor of the day.

Now look in the back of God's Book in Revelation 3:14, and we find that the church of this last part of the church age had been just so prophesied. He reminds us here that Christ is still 'the great Amen, the faithful and true Witness, the beginning of the creation of God.'

Then in the following verses the Lord decries the nauseating lukewarmness of the church in this Laodicean age. Though the church of this period has more riches and goods than ever before, it does not know that in the Lord's eyes it is "wretched, and miserable, and poor, and blind, and naked" (Rev. 3:17).

Then in verse 18 God counsels the church to buy of Him gold tried in the fire and white raiment (to be clothed with purity) and eyesalve so that we can once again see what we ought to be in His sight.

In verse 19 He calls for this church of the latter days to repent. When we see the theatrical programs and the mod, contemporary and worldly music in many of these churches, it seems not surprising to see the Lord *outside* of the church in verse 20, asking for admittance!

Thank God, as the chapter ends, we find that there will still be overcomers who will, even in these days of apostasy and compromise, share His victory and sit down with the Father in His throne!

(4) *Will souls be saved on earth after the tribulation begins?*

Yes. From chapter 4 of Revelation until chapter 19, we are given the details of the things that shall be "hereafter" upon the earth. While every saved soul on earth when Jesus comes will have been taken up by the Bridegroom at the rapture of the church, we still find a multitude out of all nations and kindreds and people and tongues standing before the throne in Revelation 7:9; and we soon find that they have come out of the Great

Tribulation and have washed their robes and made them white in the blood of the Lamb (see vs. 14). Just before that, the Lord will have sealed 144,000 Jews from out of the tribes of Israel; so it would appear that the multitude saved out of the tribulation will have been saved because of the witness of the 144,000 Jews.

People alive on earth now had better not be so foolish as to think they can wait and be saved during the tribulation. God will be working in an entirely different way in that day. Now people can be saved by grace through faith in the finished work of Christ and have the instant and certain assurance of everlasting life. It would appear that to be saved during the tribulation will bring not only the agonizing calamities of that judgment period upon their heads but that they will eventually be killed as martyrs in that day (see the last verses of chap. 13).

(5) *Does the present ecology face disaster as some fear?*

In Revelation, chapter 8, verse 7, hail and fire, mingled with blood, will be cast upon the earth, and a third part of the trees will be burned up, and all green grass will be burned up. Whether this happens by direct angelic dispatch or through the atomic wars that are threatening civilization today remains to be seen. In succeeding verses we find a great mountain burning with fire cast into the sea and the third part of the sea becoming blood, a third of the creatures in the sea destroyed and a third of all ships demolished. Following that, a third of all rivers (vs. 10) become bitter with wormwood (vs. 11). In verse 12 we find that the sun, moon and stars also will be greatly affected. Yes, the ecology will take a licking, but again it is because of the judgment of God on human sin.

(6) *Will terrifying disaster and great danger bring men to repentance?*

No. In chapter 9 of Revelation we see that horrible creatures will be unleashed and brought up out of a bottomless pit to torment men. No science-fiction thriller that has ever been written can even come near the terrible encounters that men will have with these grotesque beings. Yet, in spite of all this, they "repented not of the works of their hands, that they should not worship devils. . . . Neither repented they of their murders, nor of their sorceries, nor of their fornication, nor of their thefts" (Rev. 9:20,21). Disaster will not convert men. Only the Spirit of God and the Word of God can accomplish this (Rom. 10:17).

(7) *Why is the tribulation period called the time of Jacob's trouble?*

Because this is particularly a time of judgment for the Jewish people as God puts them in the crucible and brings to birth a new age of conversion for them. The travail of the tribulation precedes this birth. Revelation 11:2 finds Jerusalem trodden under foot of the Gentiles for forty-two months (3½ years). Two Jewish witnesses (obviously Moses and Elijah) will return to bear witness to the truth for "a thousand, two hundred and threescore days" (Rev. 11:3). Verse 6 identifies these two Israelites who will be slain by the beast of prophecy (vs. 7) when their testimony has been finished.

Satellite television is one very possible explanation of verse 9, which tells us that people of all nations will be able to see their dead bodies lie in the streets of Jerusalem. People will be so thrilled to have the voices of God's servants silenced that they will rejoice and send gifts one to another, much as we do now to celebrate Christmas (vs. 10).

Sinners would rather be tormented by horrible creatures and great disasters than to be tormented by hearing the Word of God. What a commentary on Jeremiah 17:9! After 3½ days of lying dead in the streets, God will raise His two witnesses, and they will go up to Heaven in a cloud (vs. 12). This will be nothing new for Elijah! And as for Moses, no one ever knew what became of his body anyway!

In chapter 12 we find Satan still persecuting the woman (Israel) who brought Jesus into this world. Satan (the great red dragon of vs. 3) is the one who inspired Herod the king to seek the life of Christ as soon as He was born (see vs. 4). Satan knew that this Jesus was born to rule all nations (vs. 5). The Devil has always been after the nation Israel, hence one fiendish attack after another on the Jews, from Pharaoh to Haman to Herod to Hitler, and right on up into the agonizing days of the Great

Tribulation; for here we find the woman (Israel) fleeing into the wilderness (vs. 6) to be miraculously preserved of God. So God will allow Satan to persecute Israel (vs. 13) and try to completely drown her during the tribulation, and then especially declare war on the remnant of believing Jews (vs. 17).

(8) *Who is the beast and what is his mark?*

The beast of Revelation 13 is a Satan-possessed man who will attract attention and worship of the world, even as God's Son, the Lord Jesus, drew the worship of those who would be saved. The biblical Trinity is God the Father, God the Son, and God the Holy Spirit. Satan's trinity (always the great counterfeiter, imitator and mimic) is the Devil, the Beast and the False Prophet. The beast is also called Antichrist, the man of sin, the wicked, a vile person and the lawless one, among other names. He will, for awhile, be the world dictator.

The dragon (Satan) gives the beast *his* power (vs. 2), even as Jesus ministered in the power of *God.* All the world will wonder after and worship this Satan-man. The world has been looking for a world leader, someone who can bring world peace and solve their problems. Refusing Christ, God's perfect Man, the race will accept the Devil's man.

This beast will have great power given unto him, and he will speak many blasphemies against God. False religions and the evil spirit of the times are already preparing the world for this. He will have power and authority over all the people of the earth (vs. 7) and will especially direct his hatred and wrath against the saints of God—the believing Jews and others who become saved during the tribulation. Others, those whose names are not written in the Lamb's book of life (vs. 8), will worship this great political and religious leader as if he were God in person.

The false prophet of verses 11 to 16 will perform miracles and great wonders in order to make the lost multitudes worship the beast and thus surrender their souls to Satan. So the false prophet will do for the beast much of what the Holy Spirit does for Jesus.

The *mark* of the beast will be a lasting and indelible mark which all sinners in that day will take either in their right hand or in their forehead, which is their computer "OK" to buy and sell under the reign of the beast. There will also be a number given to these same people.

Satan has gradually been getting us all used to numbers: serial numbers, code numbers, Social Security numbers, credit card numbers, bank card numbers, and many more. How simple it will be when people are told to take one more number so they can buy groceries. Out goes their hand; the number is imprinted, and their doom is sealed! This is the mark of the beast—(Rev. 13:16-18). How much better to receive the Lord Jesus Christ now, before the rapture; then you will not be here to face the agonizing days of the beast!

(9) *What and when is Armageddon?*

In Revelation 14 to 16 we have the climax days of the Great Tribulation, God thrusting His sickle into the earth to reap the harvest of wickedness (14:15-19). In verse 20, blood is seen flowing in a river that reaches up to the bridles of the horses. The winepress of the wrath of Almighty God is thus trod (see Joel 3:13,14). Angels come in chapter 15 of Revelation with the "seven last plagues; for in them is filled up the wrath of God" (vs. 1). Observe that this is a "sign in heaven" and that there will be many there at that time who have "gotten the victory over the beast, and over his image, and over his mark, and over the number of his name" (vs. 2). Some of these will be converted (and martyred) Jews singing the song of Moses (vs. 3), and some will be saved and martyred Gentiles singing the song of the Lamb of God. All will be singing the praise of Him who loved us and gave Himself for us.

In Revelation 16 the last plagues, the vials of wrath, are poured out upon a God-hating, Christ-rejecting, sin-loving humanity. Horrible and grievous sores (vs. 2) will be visited upon those who take the mark of the beast. The seas will become as the blood of a dead man, and all life in the seas will perish (see vs. 3). Then the rivers and fountains of water become blood. Can you imagine the terror and the screaming as every faucet and fountain and spring of water suddenly spurts forth blood? Thus men will be rewarded for having persecuted and slain the saints of God and shed *their* blood (vs. 6).

Next, men will be scorched with great heat as the fourth angel pours out his vial upon the sun (vss. 8,9), but men will still not repent to give God glory!

The fifth angel will pour out his vial of wrath (vs. 10), and the earth will find itself in terrifying darkness. God will obviously withdraw the light of the sun and the moon and the stars. Perhaps this will occur in conjunction with the collapse or destruction of the world's power plants, and the earth will sink into awful darkness. On top of that, such pain will be inflicted upon men that they will literally gnaw their tongues in agony. But instead of repenting and calling upon the Lord, men will spend their hours blaspheming the name of God. This will not be surprising since profanity, obscene speech and irreverence have become commonplace in recent years. Man in that day will know nothing to do but curse!

Unclean spirits (the spirits of devils—Rev. 16:14) will then gather the kings and leaders of the whole world to the great battle of the day of Almighty God (see vs. 14), and they will be gathered into a place called Armageddon (16:16). This is "the Mount of Slaughter" where perhaps more bloody battles have been fought than any other place on earth. Armageddon is both physical and spiritual, and more. Chapter 16 speaks of the physical war, chapter 17 of the destruction of spiritual wickedness as the great Roman-Liberal-Apostate ecumenical cult is finally reduced to rubble and burned, and chapter 18 pictures the end of the economic system—the destruction of commerce. Chapter 19 presents the return of Christ in glory to finally take over and make things right.

Bible scholars have for years identified the great harlot of Revelation 17 as the Roman Catholic church. This enormous religious system has always been guilty of spiritual fornication (vs. 2). The purple and scarlet of verse 4 further identify Rome. See the full pages of purple and scarlet in the magazines when the Roman bishops, cardinals and popes are pictured. This system is full of names of blasphemy (vs. 3); and no religion has dared to be as blasphemous as Rome with its pope-worship, adoration of Mary, confessions to priests, and its declaration of salvation by works and penance in plain contradiction to what the Bible teaches about salvation by grace through faith.

This woman (the great harlot) is drunken with the blood of saints and with the blood of martyrs of Jesus (vs. 6), and no other religious system has ever murdered as many true Christians as has the church of Rome. Read history! And even in recent years has such blood been shed in Colombia, in Spain, in Mexico, and wherever Rome holds forth.

Rome is further seen in the seven mountains of verse 9, that city having always been known as the City of the Seven Hills. And no city has reigned over the kings of the earth and had such influence as Vatican City (see vs. 18). What is the one church (or religious system) that is constantly exalted on the television news and always favorably reported in the papers? Rome! No matter how unscrupulous its priests or how unscriptural its practices, it is always the priest of Rome who is the charming "good guy" on television, while the Bible-believing preacher is always pictured as a nut, a fanatic or a despised wierdo of some kind.

In recent years many churches have merged. "Protestant masses" have been observed. Many groups that once preached the Bible have given up their precious doctrines and blended in with others as the mainstream of religion moves toward Rome. "Back to the mother church" is their cry.

And now the blinded charismatics have inspired even many Christians to join forces with Rome and embrace the ecumenical movement that is moving on into the one-world church soon to be destroyed by the ten-king empire of the beast of prophecy.

On the charismatic talk shows it is not at all unusual to see "born-again" Christian Protestants sitting, laughing and "fellowshipping" with nuns and priests from the Roman church. But God still cries, "Come out of her, my people, that ye be not partakers of her sins, and that ye receive not of her plagues. For her sins have reached unto heaven, and God hath remembered her iniquities" (Rev. 18:4,5).

So while Armageddon is mentioned as such in Revelation 16, I believe that this great judgment of God actually embraces chapters 16 through 19 of the last book of the Bible.

(10) *Will we be invaded from outer space?*

Christ will return in power and great glory with the blood-washed armies of Heaven, as we find in Revelation 19:11-16. This is the only recorded earth invasion from space. The wicked will be subdued, and those who refuse to bow before the King of kings will become food for the buzzards in that day (Rev. 19:17,18). At that time the beast and the false prophet will be taken and cast into the lake of fire and brimstone (vs. 20).

(11) *Will there ever be a righteous world of peace?*

Yes, there will be when Christ reigns over the earth for a thousand years (Revelation 20); but even after that beautiful kingdom is set up and men learn what a righteous world would be like, there will still be rebellion in the human heart. Satan will have been bound by Christ in a bottomless pit (vs. 2) for the thousand-year reign. But at the end of the millennium the Devil will be released from the pit and will once more go forth to deceive the nations. Multitudes will follow him even then, proving that a forced rule of righteousness will still not change the hearts of men. In verse 10 of Revelation 20 the Devil will be taken and cast into the lake of fire along with the beast and false prophet where they will be tormented day and night forever and ever.

(12) *Is life worth living?*

The answer is in the back of the book.

Yes. Though mankind and man's plans and dreams are doomed, God has made it clear that life is gloriously worth living for those who have become the sons of God through faith in the finished work of Christ.

Revelation 21 and 22 tell us how it is all going to come out. There will be new heavens and a new earth. God will wipe away all tears. There will never again be sorrow or pain or death for those who enter His divine Heaven. Such riches and beauty as man has never imagined will be ours. The glory and honor (that which is good) from the nations of this world will be permitted there but nothing else. The gates of the city will never have to be shut. There will be no night there. Nothing will enter into that city that defiles. There will be no more curse or cursing. We shall see His face and we will serve Him.

This will be the character of the everlasting life God has promised. It will be real. It will be glorious. It will never end. And it can be yours right now by faith as you submit to the truth of the Word of God and trust the Lord Jesus Christ to become your Saviour!

Bread for Believers

By Dr. Curtis Hutson

Believer is a common word in the day and age in which we live. But do we really understand the meaning of this important word? Dr. Hutson asks, "What Is a Believer?" in the first chapter of his beautiful new book published by the Sword of the Lord. He carefully answers this question for the reader.

From his original question to the close of the book, he covers the subject completely and thoroughly. You will read about the believer's security, commission, criticism, trouble, chastening, need, responsibility, hope, judgment, knowing God's will, and Heaven, the home of the believers.

This volume would be a wonderful gift for any new believer and should be found on the library shelf of every born-again Christian to be used as a refresher course from time to time. The lovely cover first attracts your eye, but the content comes across with power, doctrinal truths, and warm compassion.

Dr. Hutson's messages are as inspiring in print as they are from the pulpits of America. Get this brand new book right away to enjoy and share with others.